THE SHOCKING HISTORY OF PEE

Ronald H Blumer

Middlemarch Media Press
2017

To my loving and ever-tolerant wife.

Published by:

M_mP

Middlemarch Media Press

New York, NY 10024

blumer@middlemarch.com

ISBN-13: 978-1548712877

ISBN-10: 1548712876

Copyright © 2017 Middlemarch Media Press

The text of this book has been registered with the Writer's Guild of America, Registration number I-301452

Vb26

Speaking of existential angst... I noticed that a lot of people in government kept saying things like, "What gets me out of bed in the morning is making sure our veterans have good jobs," or "What gets me out of bed in the morning is seeing to it that every child in America has a world-class education, or "What gets me out of bed in the morning is doing everything I can to see that our electric grid is secure."

I thought to myself, "Why is everyone in this town so depressed?" What gets me out of bed in the morning is having to pee.[1]

Senator Al Franken

PISSING AT THE MOON
Pieter Brueghel the Younger 1564-1638

CONTENTS

PREFACE 6
PEE PRIMER 9
PRAYERS & POTIONS 20
PRE-INDUSTRIAL PRODUCTION 45
PISS PROPHETS 60
PHOSPHORUS 83
PISSOIRS 89
PLEASURE & PERVERSION 117
PISS ART 131
POSTSCRIPT 156
BIBLIOGRAPHY 158
NOTES 159

PREFACE

Why me?!

There have been weighty, best-selling books written on the subjects of salt, sugar, oxygen, beer, cod, and gold, so why not a book on a golden liquid that has been equally seminal to the story of civilization? But with all the scholars in all the universities in all the world desperately searching for a poem or a butterfly or a clause in the law to tear apart and then inflate into a five-hundred-page, heavily-footnoted monograph, why is it left to me to spend my life up to my elbows in the smelly detritus of history?

The author contemplating his Mayan muse

A little background. I am a filmmaker who has made several dozen non-X-rated documentaries on American history. By its very nature, film is very concrete–you have to show stuff on the screen. Working in that medium required me to research the history of everyday life–what people ate, what chairs and other furniture they rested their backsides on, how they dressed—even what kind of underwear they wore or didn't wear. Off screen, I became curious about the many other unmentionable ordinaries of everyday life. For example, how did people clean their rears before the invention of paper? Pursuing this noble quest, I went to the vast research library on Fifth Avenue in New York and discovered, to my astonishment, that there were no books on that subject—none—not even books on the invention of toilet paper a huge industry. Well, thought I, here is a virgin field for serious scholarship, and I produced the 207-page epic, *WIPED, The Curious History of Toilet Paper* complete with illustrations that left nothing to the imagination. Although never a best seller, the book rose very high on some very esoteric Google search lists.

But the question remains: Why me? Why must I, and not some bearded scholar, fill this void? The answer is simple; the subject is distasteful. A Ph.D. thesis on the semiology of urine, or, for that matter, on the semiology of any liquid or solid secreted by the human body, in not likely to put an aspiring professor on the fast track for a tenured position at Harvard. I experienced a similar resistance to my ass-wiping masterwork. One rejection letter from an agent highly praised the manuscript's style and thorough scholarship but concluded with this memorable sentence, "I hope that someday you find a courageous publisher."

In fact, this bottom-up view of the world did reveal some truly fascinating historical gems. I discovered that Henry VIII and subsequent kings had their personal, human ass wipers–high court positions. I also found out that the ancient Greeks used stones for the job, three if they were rough, four if they were smooth, and I uncovered the portrait of a man who almost became Pope by kissing his patron's freshly wiped ass.

Which brings me to the subject of urine. What a story this lowly product of our innards has to tell! And yet, even in the bowels of the vast Library of Congress, not one serious history of pee graces its shelves.

It seems that it is again up to me to clean out the Augean Stables of academia. I am no Hercules, but as I, and (I hope) you, patient reader will discover, this familiar liquid runs its fascinating course through all of history – playing a major role in war, religion, industry, fine arts, medicine, cosmetics, as well as strange sexual practices, the origin of vampires, and a distressing US Supreme Court decision affecting all of our rights to privacy.

So, to paraphrase Sir Isaac Newton, let us prepare ourselves for this great if slightly odiferous ocean of truth that lies undiscovered before us.

TWO
PEE PRIMER

At 1:12 AM on Thursday, June 16, 2011, in Portland, Oregon, a twenty-one-year-old lad had to go–the most commonplace of needs. Unfortunately for the Portland economy, he climbed a fence and 'went' in the 50-million-gallon reservoir that supplies the city with its drinking water. Even more unfortunately, his urinary transgression was caught on surveillance video. This being the age of the Internet, the blurry image of the young man urinating went viral, creating an outcry that forced the city to drain the reservoir. This action cost the taxpayers of Portland $32,700. When asked about this situation, David Shaff, administrator for the Water Bureau explained that, although he regularly finds dead animals rotting in the huge reservoir,

"this is different." When challenged on the scientific basis for being concerned about such a small amount of urine affecting such a huge reservoir, Shaff answered, "It has nothing to do with science. Do you want to drink pee!?"[2]

The startling answer to Mr. Shaff's rhetorical question will be dealt with at length in the next chapter of this book. Suffice it to say that:

a) drinking pee is not harmful
b) the boy's pee in Portland's water would be chemically undetectable, and
c) human beings really are weird.

Locusts in trees do it
The bees do it
Even over-educated fleas do it
Let's do it, let's fall in love!

Cole Porter's witty lyrics reminds us that in "doing it" we are one with nature and all of humanity. Another thing we all do is pee. To Descartes's famous dictum, 'I think, therefore I am,' I can add my own less elegant, "we wee, therefore we be." If we are healthy, we wee several times a day; while fish and animals without bladders do it continuously. It is such a commonplace activity that we don't think much about it, and most of us don't write books celebrating this activity.

Of all the stuff that spews out of our body, urine is the most benign. As the reservoir story illustrates, we don't all warmly embrace its golden benignity, but we don't regard it with the same strong repugnance that we bestow on the other contenders in the field – say vomit or snot. We don't have many statues of people shitting or vomiting (except perhaps in the more advanced salons of the avant-garde,) but we do have statues of pishers, the most famous of which is situated in what must be one of the more uptight cities the world, Brussels, Belgium. Most people think that it's very cute to see a little boy tinkling. And so that half of humanity would not be left out of the fun, in 1987, the city commissioned a two-foot bronze statue of a sweet little girl, her hair in short bronze pigtails, squatting and peeing on a blue-grey limestone base. Her official name is *Jeanneke Pis*, and she pees right down the street from her more famous brother.

Our reaction to these images mirrors the reality that pee is a much higher-class, sophisticated stuff than its truly unpleasant neighbor–poop. In the production of excrement, like all vertebrates, we have, in effect, one tube that goes from our mouth to our anus. And what happens in-between is highly unpleasant. First, our croissant or filet mignon gets mulched and dissolved in the strong acids of the stomach, squeezed dry in the small intestine, and then attacked and further broken down by really nasty bacteria in the large intestine. It is not surprising that what comes out the other end is a smelly mess.

If we can compare the body's production of feces to a rotting compost heap, our creation of urine is the biological equivalent of a Mozart concerto. Urine is a by-product of blood. Textbooks tell us that our blood is filtered through the liver and the kidneys and then dripped into the bladder to be excreted as soon as we locate the nearest bathroom or tree. But the word 'filtered' does not do justice to the highly complex route from blood to pee. Every minute, one-quarter of our blood supply passes through the liver/kidney system. There, useful nutrient components such as amino acids, and glucose are added to the blood, and dead cells are removed. Poisons are not only removed but neutralized. What happens then is more akin to balancing than to filtering. If we have too much potassium or too little phosphorus, the kidneys minutely rebalance our blood adding and or subtracting just the right ingredients before sending out blood on another quick trip around our entire system to return for another session of re-processing. Forty gallons of our blood is processed to make the quart or so of the urine we whiz out in a day. When pee emerges from a healthy body into the outside world in all its yellow glory, it is 95% water and completely sterile. Only a tiny fraction of this transformation from blood to pee can truly be called a waste product.

Some of this waste comes from the breakdown of proteins in our used-up blood. Normally, decomposed protein would become ammonia–the stuff in cleaning fluid and a deadly corrosive poison. The advanced factory in our liver cleverly locks up this poison in a complex chemical compound called urea, which we then can safely piss out without dissolving our pissers. Kidney failure or liver disease results in a build-up in our blood of urea and other bad stuff. Without drastic medical intervention such as dialysis, we would soon be dead.

The rest is just plumbing, including the bladder, an expandable bag to hold the output dripping from the kidneys, and the urethra, a tube that carries that liquid to the outside world.

In males, part of this urethra does double duty, as explained by the character played by Peter O'Toole in the movie *My Favorite Year*. In one scene, dead drunk, he staggers into the ladies' bathroom and is confronted by a woman:

> **Lil:** *Sir, this is for ladies only!!*
>
> **Peter O'Toole** [unzipping his fly]: *So is <u>this</u>, ma'am, but every now and then I have to run a little water through it.*

Outside of the body, bacteria breaks down the urea dissolved in our urine turning it back into ammonia. The pungent smell of ammonia is one of the compounds that gives the New York subway system its distinctive fragrance.

Urea is the major chemical dissolved in the water of our urine, comprising about 2.5% of our pee. Urea is also the main ingredient in fertilizers and a chemical with dozens of other uses.[3] We manufacture urea in complex chemical factories–two hundred million tons of urea each year–more than any other organic chemical We then eat our urea-grown food on tables and tableware also made with urea, because the chemical is also made into a form of plastic used in unbreakable plates and cups and on the Formica surface of our tables and kitchen counters. Urea is all around us, from the laminate in our floors to the insulation and soundproofing in our walls, from glues to compounds that reduce pollution generated by trucks and factories. And, in the following pages, you will discover that we brush our teeth with it, wash our hair with it, and liberally smear the stuff on our skin. Finally, harkening back to its urinary roots, urea supplies the pigment in inks, paints. and plastics with the color–what else– yellow.

The urea in our pee once played a decisive role in the history of science. Until the early 19th century, scientists were convinced that there were two kinds of substances in the world, the chemicals of life, produced by animals and plants, and chemicals of the earth, such as rocks and salt. The theory was called vitalism–the belief that living organisms possessed an unknown 'vital force' that allowed them to create what are known as organic chemicals. This theory was exploded by a German chemist, Friedrich Wohler. In 1828, he synthesized urea by using off-the-shelf chemicals. In a flash, he realized that rocks and salt and our beating hearts are all just different combinations of ordinary chemicals. Writing to a fellow researcher, he was so excited that he metaphorically peed in his pants, "I cannot, so to say, hold my chemical water and must tell you that I can make urea without needing the kidneys of an animal, be it human or dog!" Wohler knew that he had made a discovery that would change our understanding of the world forever.

Apart from water and urea, the other 2.5% of our urine is a chemistry-set-mixture of salts and complex molecules. Urochrome from the breakdown of the hemoglobin in our blood is what gives normal pee its distinctive yellowish color. Because of the efficiency of the kidneys in doing their job, our pee also carries a precise inventory of all the body's chemical, metabolic, and drug-taking activities. This explains why we have that awkward pee–in–the–cup session at the doctor's office, and also why the careers of some of the world's top athletes have come to an abrupt end.

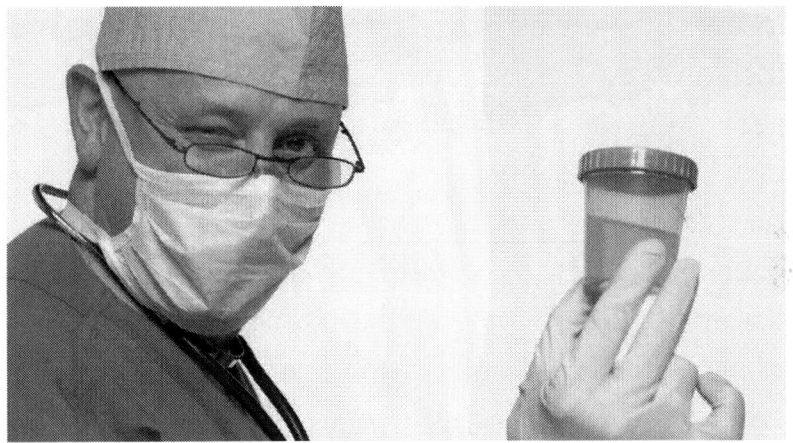

Several years ago, author Paul Spinrad conducted an unofficial survey and came up with some fun pee stats.[4] We all pee five to seven times a day, depending on age and how long we spend in the pub. Spinrad found that some people actually time their pissing with a stopwatch; sixteen-year-old student claims an astounding record of two minutes forty seconds. (Most of us would be proud to reach the one-minute mark.) Sixty percent of Spinrad's respondents admit to peeing in the shower—an undercount, I suspect—while fourteen percent of males claimed they urinated from a moving car. That figure may be high because the survey was taken in car-crazy California.

He also reported that sixty-seven percent of his subjects admitted to peeing in a swimming pool. We now have a very precise method of measuring the ratio of pee to water at your local 'Y.' A brilliant researcher from the University of Alberta, Xing-Fang Li, realized that artificial sweeteners pass right through you—from Coke to pee to pool.[5] Measure the amount of saccharine in the water and, according to Dr. Li, "you have a good proxy for pee." Li's team collected water from pools and hot tubs at hotels and recreation facilities in several Canadian cities. The results: in a commercial-sized swimming pool, you are floating in about 20 gallons of pee. If you have any doubt about the accuracy of Dr. Li's measurements, here is a distressing fact which, as my late mother would put it, "Better you shouldn't know." The strong chlorine smell in an indoor swimming pool comes not from the disinfecting compound added to the water, which is itself odorless. The smell comes from the chemical reaction between this compound and the gallons of pee added to the pool by its innocent-looking occupants.[6]

One final pee fact: because everything in pee comes from life, it is very useful to life. The average American pulls the flush lever five to seven times a day; each flush sends under a cup or two of pee mixed with a few gallons of water into the sewer. Not only is this liquid rich in the fertilizer urea, but it also contains a phosphorus compound–another essential chemical that makes plants grow. Unfortunately, as author Carol Steinfeld tells us, this fertilizing pee ends up growing destructive algae in our waterways, killing fish and poisoning the seashore. She points out that, instead of being "pissed away," the approximately 90 million gallons of urine that Americans produce each year, has enough nitrogen to fertilizer 12 million acres of corn."[7] Why go to the expense of manufacturing urea when we are literally swimming in the stuff? Fortunately, most other countries recognize the real value of their excrement, and they value pee as a very useful resource. Some people call it liquid gold.

THREE
PRAYERS & POTIONS

In June 1978, newspapers featured the very latest in women's fashion–blazers of flocked nylon, a fabric that looked like velvet. *Happy Days* and *Little House on Prairie* were among the most popular shows on network television (the only kind of television there was). *Grease,* starring John Travolta, was the highest grossing musical of the decade and the Bee Gees were more than *Stayin' Alive*, selling millions of vinyl phonograph disks. Newspaper readers were riveted by the trial of serial killer David Berkowitz, dubbed 'The Son of Sam.' Somewhere, buried on the back pages, a few might read about the visit to the United States of the aged and aggressively uncharismatic Prime Minister of India, Morarji Desai.

His obscurity would dramatically change on Sunday, June 4, 1978. During an interview on the widely-watched CBS news program *60 Minutes*, Dan Rather, vainly attempting to stay awake, threw at Mr. Desai the following soft-ballest of softball questions. It was the sort of question you ask an important person when you can't think of anything else to say:

> **Rather:** Tell us how are you able to run the government of India, working 12 hours a day or more, horseback riding in the countryside, talking vigorously in public at the age of 82 years young. Tell us your secret.
>
> **Desai:** My diet consists of fruit and vegetable juices, fresh and natural milk, plain yogurt, honey, fresh fruits, raw nuts, five cloves of garlic every day...

At this point, the poor producers of *60 Minutes* must have been desperate to liven things up by cutting to a commercial for tires or anti-dandruff shampoo. But then Desai added the following:

> **Desai:**...and I drink five to eight ounces of urine every morning on an empty stomach.

At this point, Dan Rather lost his journalist's cool.

> **Rather:** Yack! You drink your urine? That is the most repulsive thing I have ever heard!

This was perhaps the one and only time that this consummately professional reporter ever used the word 'yack' when interviewing a foreign dignitary. Desai went on to open the eyes and drop the jaws of Americans with this short urinary primer.

> **Desai:** Don't be alarmed, it is a very natural treatment. In my country mothers used to give babies their own urine when they were suffering from a stomach ache. And in Hindu philosophy, cow's urine has been considered holy, and it is prescribed in every ceremony. Drinking urine fights the cause of all diseases, and it costs you nothing. So, people drink their urine. Many medicines are worse in color, taste, and smell, but still people take them. You should taste it to find out.

Dan Rather "respectfully" declined the offer, and most viewers were, in turn, shocked, disgusted or amused. But the secret was now out. Not only was guzzling a cup of your own pee in the morning as Indian as apple pie, but this imbibing had been an accepted activity on the subcontinent for at least 5,000 years.

Desai was a proponent of the regimen called Urine Therapy or UT for short. The author J. D. Salinger was a disciple, as was India's founding father Mahatma Gandhi and the Brazilian martial arts fighter Lyoto Machida, also known as '*The Dragon.*' The movie star Sarah Miles drank her own urine for 30 years. UT enthusiasts promise not only good health but longevity. Desai and Salinger lived to the age of 91. Gandhi was in excellent health when he was assassinated at 78. The Brazilian dragon, only in his late 30s, presumably still has many more years to go.

Urine Therapy is a movement combining the world of alternative medicine with the enthusiasm of a religious cult. Evidence points to the fact that human beings have been using this product coming out of their bodies in and on their bodies since the beginning of recorded time. Both European peasantry and native cultures around the world have been convinced that it has great healing power when used appropriately.

John Gregory Bourke was an American anthropologist with a strange obsession (but who am I to judge). In 1891, he published an extraordinary study, *Scatologic Rites of All Nations*.[8] In this book, he witnessed and described, without any of the usual academic dispassion, a urine-drinking ceremony performed by the Zuni, a Southwest tribe of Native Americans:

> As they were finishing their dance, this squaw entered, carrying a pot of urine, of which the filthy brutes drank heartily. I refused to believe the evidence of my senses and asked Cushing if that were really human urine. "'Why, certainly," replied he, "and here comes more of it." This time it was a large tin pail full, not less than two gallons. I was standing by the squaw as she offered me this strange and abominable refreshment. She made a motion

with her hand to indicate to me that it was urine, and one of the old men repeated the Spanish word *mear* (to urinate), while my sense of smell demonstrated the truth of their statements. The dancers swallowed great draughts, smacked their lips, and, amid the roaring merriment of the spectators, remarked that it was very, very good. To this outline description of their disgusting rite, I have little to add.

In another publication, he reported that followers of folk medicine in America and Europe believed that, after a woman had just given birth, drinking the urine of her husband would help her expel the placenta. He also noted, with his typical disgust, that Mexicans would regularly rub the warm urine of a young boy on their hands and faces to improve their complexions and to remove blemishes. As we shall discover later in this chapter, this treatment is actually effective.

One of the most ancient Hindu Sanskrit works, *The Damar Tantra,* contains a detailed description of a practice called *Shivambu Kalpa Vidhi* (drinking urine to rejuvenate) as expounded by one of the most important gods in Hinduism, Lord Shiva. Shiva's detailed instructions on how this rite is to be performed leaves nothing to chance.

> 1) One's own urine should be collected in a utensil made of clay or better yet of copper.
>
> 2) The intending practitioner of the therapy should abjure salty or bitter foods, should not over-exert himself, should take a light meal in the evening, should sleep on the ground, and should control and master his senses.
>
> 3) The sagacious practitioner should get up when three-quarters of the night have elapsed and should pass urine while facing the east.
>
> 4) The wise one should leave out the first and the last portions of the urine, and collect only the middle portion.
>
> 5) The practitioner of Yoga should take this heavenly nectar before proceeding with his other rituals.[9]

Follow these rules, and you will be cured of all diseases. And that is just for starters. The Tantra also explains:

> One who drinks Shivambu for the duration of a month will be purified internally. Drinking it for two months stimulates and energizes the senses. Drinking it for three months destroys all diseases and frees one from all troubles. By drinking it for five months, one acquires divine vision. Continuation of the practice for six months makes the practitioner highly intelligent and proficient in the Scriptures, and if the duration is seven months, the practitioner acquires extraordinary strength. If the practice is continued for eight months, one acquires a permanent glow like

that of gold, ten months of this practice makes one a veritable treasury of luster. Eleven months of it would purify all the organs of the body. A man who has continued the practice for a year becomes the equal of the sun in radiance. He who has continued for two years conquers the element Earth. If the practice is continued for three years, one conquers the element of Water, and if it is continued for four years, the element of Light is also conquered. He who continues the practice for five years conquers the element Air, and he who continues it for seven years conquers pride. Continuation of the practice for eight years enables one to conquer all the important elements of Nature, and continuation of it for nine years frees one from the cycle of birth and death. One who has continued the practice for ten years can fly through the air without effort. One who has continued it for eleven years is able to hear the voice of his inner self. He who has continued the practice for twelve years will live so long as the moon and the stars last. He is not troubled by dangerous animals such as snakes, and no poisons can kill him. He cannot be consumed by fire and can float on water just like wood.[10]

With this promise as part of Hindu liturgy, it is not surprising that UT has its most staunch supporters in present-day India. Dozens of books published in the subcontinent preach the gospel of pee; government departments promote the practice; and passionate advocates echo Lord Shiva's promise that UT will bring everything from perfect health to immortality. One author, Dr. G. K Takkar, whose business card lists him as Chairman of India's

Water of Life Foundation and a tax consultant, claims that drinking your urine will cure your fear of public speaking. C.S. Rayudu also multitasks as an expert in media and public relation as well as a UT promoter. Here is the front cover of his book:

The back cover of this book promises that the book will be "straight forward, precise and to the point. No bull !!"[11] In this work, he explains that the "miracle juice affects the energy fields of the body, correcting imbalances in these internal bio-fields to reinstate health." He lists just some of the diseases and conditions it can treat:

Urine therapy prevents or cures ailments, enhances, improves longevity, cleans bowels, intestines, alimentary canal, improves the quality of the skin. It is effective against the flu, common cold, broken bones, whitening teeth, toothache and ocher mouth problems, dry skin, psoriasis, sinus, skin diseases, cancer, aids, cardiovascular complaints, allergies, animal and snake bites, asthma, bronchitis, hypertension, burns, wounds, injuries, chemical intoxication, chickenpox, enteritis, constipation, pneumonia, dysentery, edema, eczema, eye irritation, conjunctivitis, sight disorders, fatigue, gonorrhea, gout, blood urine, smallpox, immunological disorders, infections, infertility, baldness, insomnia, jaundice, hepatitis, Kaposi's sarcoma, leprosy, lymphatic disorder, urticaria, morning sickness, hangover, nasal disorders, congestions, obesity, papilloma virus, opportunistic infections associated with VDS, HIV, parasitosis, respiratory disorders, gastric ulcer, rheumatism, birthmarks, strokes, lumbago, typhus, gastritis, cold sores, tuberculosis, tetanus, foot fungus, endocrine-related diseases, ulcerative colitis, pelvic inflammatory diseases, adrenal, digestive problems, exhaustion, excessive weakness, menstruation disorders, miscarriage, prostate trouble, arthritis, glaucoma, cataract, malaria, diphtheria, scarlet fever, scurvy, bed wetting, mucous colitis, pyorrhea, gangrene, etc.[12]

Dr. Rayudu specifies the following methods to use this panacea:

1) **Oral.** Many have a problem drinking urine because of its color, taste and smell. Hence, they

hesitate. Come on, drink up your nectar juice! It is like manna from heaven.

2) **Massaging** to relieve muscle pain and skin disorders.

3) **Sniffling** for colds and coughs. While breathing urine through the nose, you will enjoy the smell.

4) **Bathing.** Better than a bubble bath as it is more hygienic and antiseptic. We spend too much money on creams and lotions. With urine, we do not need soap or shampoo All disorders disappear, and skin becomes soft and shining.

5) **Injecting**. When urine is injected with a syringe, it is like injecting fuel, energy, force, nutrients, and hormones into the body. Dr. Salaria in Ahmedabad regularly injects urine into his patients before performing major surgery.

6) **Enema.** A urine enema sweeps out poisonous materials from the body.

Rayudu admits that pee is not a cure-all. On page 245, he lists several exceptions, saying that drinking or dunking yourself or even inserting this "divine nectar" up your rear will *not* cure stress or depression. He also specifies that UT will not help a patient on his or her death bed, or with what he rather poetically calls, "diseases of impossibilities." Finally, Dr. Rayudu reminds us that urine will do absolutely nothing to improve your karma. These exceptions noted, his impassioned conclusion is to "stay out of the physician's office, instead use your own body's medicine. We may not understand the mysteries of the Creator's power. His ways are not our ways. Drink and believe!"

This cult of pee drinking has followings in other countries, including Great Britain and the United States. The China Urine Therapy Association was founded by Mr. Bao Yafu in Hong Kong in 2008.

Every morning Mr. Bao heads to the roof terrace of his cluttered office to enjoy a fresh cup of his own urine with a nice head of foam on top. An athletic 80-year-old, he has been drinking his own urine for 45 years and is an inspiration to the younger members of his association.

The Chinese branch of UT also promotes the idea that pee is a cure-all for everything that ails you from baldness to cancer. For example, Mr. Bao bathes his eyes in urine. "I do this when I wake up," he says. "I am an old man, but my vision is perfect. You can do so many things with urine; I wash my face with it, I soak my ears in it and, of course, it is the ideal shampoo for my hair."

Mr. Bao is only the latest example of how various people have used pee throughout the ages to treat a wide spectrum of illnesses. *Naturalis Historia*, one of the largest single works to have survived from the Roman Empire, purports to cover the entire field of ancient knowledge "based on the best authorities." It was written by Pliny the Elder who died in AD 79 during the eruption of Vesuvius. Reading this massive work, even the modern reader inured to the chaos of the Internet will be overwhelmed by this collection of miscellany compiled by Pliny two thousand years ago. Its list of 20,000 'facts,' is a mixture of science, chemistry, magic, ancient folk medicine, and fantasy. Among the cures and potions, urine is ubiquitous. Here is a sampling:

> § At Corinth, there is a tree which the Greeks call 'brya.' There is a story told, that, mixed with the urine of an ox it will act most effectually to suppress the flames of desire. The magicians say that the urine of a eunuch will have a similar effect. A lizard

drowned in a man's urine will also have the effect of an anti-aphrodisiac upon the person whose urine it is.

§ A plant upon which a dog has watered, torn up by the roots, and not touched with iron, is a very speedy cure for sprains

§ The urine of children who have not arrived at puberty is a sovereign remedy for the cure of films and marks upon the eyes, and maladies of the eyelids. In combination with the meal of fitches, it is used for the cure of burns, and, with a head of a leek, it is boiled down to one-half, in a new earthen vessel, for the treatment of suppurations of the ears, or the extermination of worms breeding in those organs. The vapor of this decoction stimulates menstruation.

§ Stale urine: some mix ashes of calcined oyster shells, as a liniment for corrosive sores, burns, and diseases of the rectum. The most celebrated midwives have pronounced that there is no lotion which removes itching sensations more effectually.

§ The fact is, and there is no impropriety in saying so, that every person's own urine is the best for his own case, due care being taken to apply it immediately, and unmixed with anything else in such cases as the quill of a hedgehog entering the flesh, a sponge or some wool being the vehicle with which it is applied. Kneaded up with ashes, it is good for the bite of a mad dog. As to the bite of a centipede, the effects of urine are said to be quite marvelous—the person who has been injured has only to touch the crown of his head with a drop of his own urine, and he will experience an instantaneous cure. For a painful cramp, the urine of a she-goat, injected into the ears, is found to be very useful.

Pliny also noted that urine is very effective at removing ink stains from your toga. (After writing the 37 books of his encyclopedia, he should know.)

Despite Pliny's claims for urine's curative powers, this polymath Roman showed a distinctly modern reluctance to fully engage in UT:

> I should hesitate in giving circulation to a prescription for injuries inflicted by the viper, were it not that Mr. Varro, then in the eighty-third year of his age, has left a statement to the effect that the most efficient remedy for the bite inflicted by this reptile is to drink his own urine.

Pliny also recommends the urine of a lynx to cure urinary infections. Ear infections can be treated by the urine of a wild boar. (I would love to know how he would suggest one goes about collecting it.) Finally, he instructs his readers on the protocols of proper peeing.

> Hesiod gives a precept, recommending persons to make water against an object standing full before them, so that no divinity may be offended by their nakedness being uncovered. Those adept in magic expressly forbid a person, when about to make water, to uncover the body in the face of the sun or moon, or to sprinkle with his urine the shadow of any object, whatsoever. Some say whoever makes water where a dog has previously watered will be sensible of numbness in the loins.

The prophet Muhammad believed that camel urine had medicinal value, and many people in the Arabian Peninsula still use it for a variety of skin problems.

It turns out that there is real science in this use of pee. For proof, you need only look into your own 21st century medicine cabinet. The active

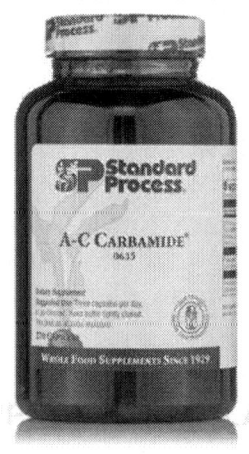
ingredient in Murine brand ear wax removal is carbamide peroxide. Carbamide is another name for urea, the main compound dissolved in the water of our urine. Carbamide is also available in health food stores in pill form marked with claims that it will "promote a healthy fluid balance in the body." The chemical is also found in shampoos and in an array of expensive skin creams. The reason; urea has the wonderful property of dissolving such bad stuff such as dead skin, dandruff, or excess ear wax, without harming the surrounding tissue. Perhaps the most surprising urinal revelation is the fact that urea is also the main ingredient of tooth whitener.

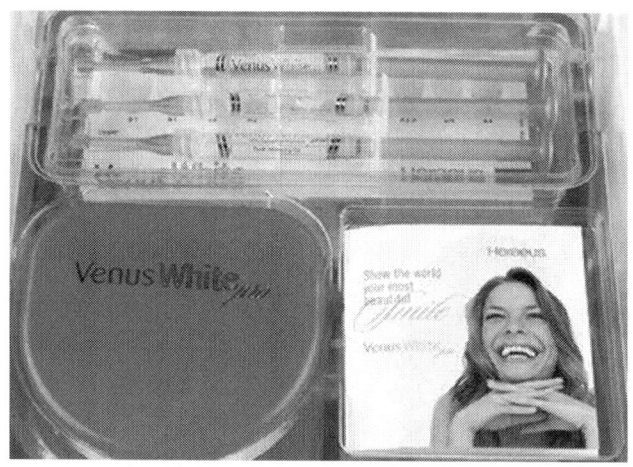

Venus White Pro Refill Kit, 16% Carbamide Peroxide Home Whitening

In ancient times, people used to get that "school girl smile" promised by advertisers simply by rubbing urine directly on their teeth. The urea in the urine removes the plaque and the ammonia does an excellent job of bleaching their teeth. History is silent on what their pee soaked breath smelled like. The great Roman satirical poet Catullus described the practice as he skewered a Spanish gentleman named of Egnatius:

> Egnatius, because he has snow-white teeth, smiles all the time. If you're a defendant in court, when the counsel draws tears, he smiles. If you're in grief at the pyre of pious sons, the lone forlorn mother weeping, he smiles. Whatever it is, wherever it is, whatever he's doing, he smiles. Now Egnatius, you are Spanish, and in the country of Spain what each man pisses, he uses to brush his teeth with, every morning. The fact that your teeth are so white and polished just shows how much you're full of piss.[13]

In Sudan, Mandari boys wash their hair in fresh cattle urine, Repeated washing with cow pee has a bleaching effect giving their hair a fashionable reddish hue. In present-day India, since cows are considered sacred, cow piss is seen to have great therapeutic properties. The manufacturer of *GoSeva Ghanavati* brand cow urine tablets advertises them as "useful for heart diseases, high blood pressure, effective in mental illnesses, a liver cleanser, blood purifier, and as a digestive aid."

Since the election in 2014 of the BJP, a Hindu Nationalist Party, India now provides major government funding for cow research, including the development and promotion of products using cow urine. Authorities are proposing the establishment of *gau vigyan*–a cow science university to further these studies. In 2017, the Indian Institute of Technology organized a workshop to investigate the "anti-cancer properties of cow urine." Cow urine research has become big business; companies have obtained patents based on cow pee's alleged therapeutic powers. Here is the description of US patents numbers 6896907 and 7235262.

> The invention relates to a novel pharmaceutical composition comprising an effective amount of bio-active fraction from cow urine distillate as a bioavailability facilitator and pharmaceutically acceptable additives selected from anticancer compounds, antibiotics, drugs, therapeutic and nutraceutic agents, ions and similar molecules which are targeted to the living systems

Unlike the urea used in Indian medicine, the urea we westerners have been popping in pills, smearing on our skin and applying to our teeth comes not from human or animal pee but from chemical sources. But what may surprise readers is the fact that, for many years, some of us have also been ingesting drugs made directly from the urine of human beings and animals. Some of these products have saved lives, and some have helped to create lives.

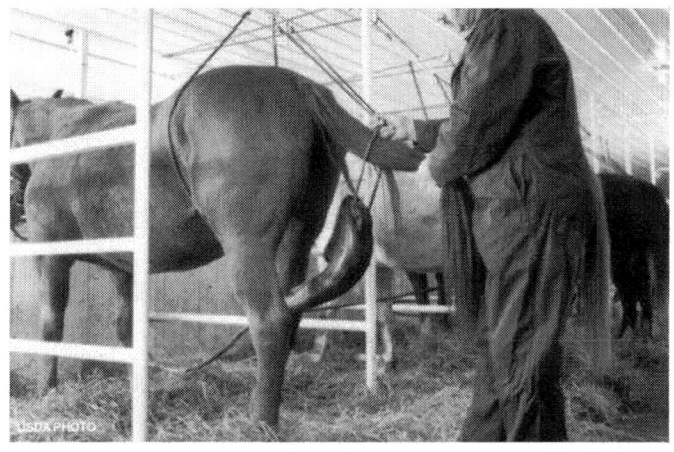

Since 1942, millions of women have been using the drug *Premarin* in the form of pills and creams to treat menopausal symptoms including hot flashes, vaginal burning, dryness, and itching. Available also as an injection, *Premarin* works by replacing the estrogen hormones that an older woman's body is no longer producing. According to the literature supplied by the drug company Wyeth Pharmaceuticals, these hormones come from unspecified "natural sources." They had no need to be so coy

37

about the fact that women were having refined horse piss injected into their bodies because the source of the hormone is built into the name: **PRE**gnant **MAr**es' ur**IN**e–voila *Premarin*. Producing this drug is a billion-dollar industry, but recently sales have declined because *Premarin* has been linked to a rise heart disease and breast cancer. Animal rights groups are also upset by reports of the cruel treatment of thousands of pregnant mares necessary to supply the tankers of horse piss from which this precious hormone is extracted.

So, as Yogis have been telling us for centuries, urine really does contain a gold mine of valuable nutrients and potential drugs. Detroit entrepreneur Earl Braxton realized the truth of this fact; and in the 1980s, his goal in life was to somehow make money from pee. He was wonderfully situated to make this dream come true because he is the owner of the *Porta John Corporation*, a company that supplies the building industry, cities, and outdoor venues with over 10,000 of those ubiquitous, very necessary, necessaries. In this capacity, Mr. Braxton had access to a steady stream of thousands of gallons of human pee. His brainwave was to form another company called *Enzymes of America* that, with wonderful synergy, would take the output from his one company and refine it into potentially lucrative products for the second.

One product that his company produced was *Urokinase*, a very pricey drug used to treat highly dangerous blood clots in the lungs. He knew that he could produce this urine-derived enzyme more economically than its synthetically manufactured equivalent. After all, the raw material was free.

Hurt in a stock market crisis and then stymied by the complex regulations controlling the introduction of new drugs, *Enzymes of America* eventually went bankrupt. Perhaps Mr. Braxton was just a pee prophet ahead of his times. He remains, however, an extremely wealthy man from *Porta John*. He has been offered millions of dollars just for the thousands of bathroom-related Internet domain names that he bought up in the 1990s. But Earl is not selling. Although frustrated by not being able to make pee pay, he is not ashamed of his profession, proudly explaining, "I'm a toilet guy."

A lower-tech version of portable toilet pee recycling has become a big hit in Denmark. The Roskilde Music Festival is the largest event of its kind in Europe, welcoming over 130,000 well-bladdered fans for eight days of beer and rock 'n' roll. As only the Danes could pull off, the micro-brewery *Nørrebro Bryghus* teamed up with Denmark's Agriculture and Food Council, and together they set up special so-called urinal zones. The resulting 13,000 gallons of youthful urine is then sprayed on fields of barley to be malted into next year's vintage of beer. Normally, the fields are grown using animal waste, but careful readers will remember that pee contains nitrogen and phosphorous compounds and is an ideal fertilizer. The brewery in no way tried to hide the golden beverage's honest roots, calling it– what else–*Pisner*.

The beer will be on sale at next year's music festival to fill yet more bladders and water more fields of barley, thus closing the ecological loop.

There is one final important story about a modern use of human pee. Curiously enough, while post-menopausal women were downing horse piss, their own urine contained an excess of very valuable hormones with the mouth-filling names of 'follicle stimulating hormone' (FSH) and 'luteinizing hormone' (LH). In 1949, an Italian scientist discovered that, when these hormones were injected into women having difficulty conceiving, the treatment stimulates them to ovulate, ultimately greatly increasing their odds of having a baby. The problem: how to mass produce this life creating miracle drug. Bruno Lunenfeld, an Austrian Jew, had a passionate interest in human fertility motivated in part by the need of Jewish people to replenish their population after the Holocaust. His description of his presentation to the drug company Serono reads like a scene from a movie:[14]

"I, just a kid, had to stand before the board of directors and ask them to help us find 400 menopausal women that would agree to collect their urine daily. I gave my lecture, they all applauded politely, and then the chairman of the board got up and said: 'Very nice, but we're a drug company, not a urine factory.' I ran out crying."

What happened next could also be in a plot from a movie. Lunenfeld was introduced to Giulio Pacelli, an Italian aristocrat and a Serono board member who took an interest in Lunenfeld's work. He returned with Lunenfeld to speak again to the board of directors. "Pacelli gave exactly the same speech I had given ten days earlier, but at the finish, he added one sentence. 'My uncle is Pope Pius XII, and he has decided to help us and to ask the nuns in old-age homes to collect their urine daily for 'a sacred cause.' That, of course, convinced the board of directors and they immediately agreed to help our research project with money and resources."

Soon, tanker trucks were hauling the pee of hundreds of nuns from Catholic retirement homes across Italy to Serono's headquarters in Rome. It would take ten peeing nuns ten days to produce enough urine for one treatment. The ovulation treatment was not only successful, but at times a little too successful, suddenly landing childless couples with a houseful of twins, triplets, or more.

Mother shaves Numbers on quadruplets heads so people can tell them apart

Today, hundreds of thousands of people walking the earth owe their very existence to the fact that their mothers or grandmothers were injected with this product made from urine. And one final twist to the story; Mr. Lunenfeld later discovered that the Vatican owned 25% of Serono Pharmaceuticals, and earned hundreds of millions of dollars from the fertility drug. The Catholic Church had discovered how to make pee pay.

Modern science now supports some of the claims of the UT proselytizers. There is indeed gold in this golden liquid. Dr. Rayudu expresses great frustration at the fact that drug companies grow rich by selling us a variety of pills and potions containing urea and the various hormones found in pee. As he reminds us frequently in his book, this 'heavenly nectar' pours out of our very own bodies. And it costs nothing.

FOUR
PRE-INDUSTRIAL PRODUCTION

Tilburg is a modern, bustling city in northern Holland, boasting three railway stations, two universities and a population of over 200,000. Everywhere in this city are drawings, souvenirs, postcards, and statues like the one above. The unhappy man with the pitcher is as much a symbol of Tilburg as the Eiffel Tower is of Paris and the Leaning Tower is of Pisa. He also appears on posters for Tilburg's annual carnival *Kruikenstat* (Jug City) held every July.

KRUIKENSTAD
Carnavalsstichting Tilburg

Visitors to this city may be surprised to learn what this man represents. His name is *Kruikezeiker* (Jug Pisser), and the pitcher he is carrying is for the collection of pee.

How does a pee collector become the symbol of a city?[15] In the 17th century, Tilburg had become a major center of Holland's wool industry. Its burghers earned their honest livings at home, spinning, weaving and finishing the cloth. As the textile industry became mechanized, Tilburg kept up with the times, boasting 145 woolen mills in the 19th century. But why pee? Today we live in a chemical world. Most things that we touch, wear, smell, and sometimes even eat are the products of complex chemical factories. But until modern times, humanity had to rely mainly on compounds that came out of the ground or directly from nature. There were no plastics, no nylon, no sodium lauryl ether sulfate, no artificial anything. But there was pee and, given the impressive beer drinking habits of this earlier age, an abundance of that liquid.

It turns out that urine, or more specifically stale, really stinky urine, was an essential ingredient in every step of wool manufacturing. Wool, as it comes off the back of a sheep, is coated with lanolin, a heavy oil that makes any further processing impossible. From ancient times until very recently, raw wool would be soaked in what a Dutch document from 1689 describes as "hot stinking piss." Attentive readers may remember that the urea in our pee, if allowed to ripen for a few days, is broken down by bacteria into ammonia, a powerful solvent of grease. The initial soaking of the wool is just the first step involving the use of urine in textile manufacturing. After the wool is woven into cloth, it undergoes a process called fulling or felting. The cloth is again immersed in a bath of 'hot stinking piss' and stomped on. The urine and a clay soil called 'fuller's earth' will absorb any remaining grease and impurities and the procedure will produce the following result, as described in a modern knitting blog. "During wool fulling, the individual fibers open up and, as the fibers are moved around, either by hand or machine, they begin to migrate and entangle with their neighbors. Wool has a magical property that can take individual threads, sometimes woven very loosely, and once in the liquid transform themselves into thick, soft cloth with great insulating properties."[16]

The wool industry created a huge demand for urine, and so, like a milkman in reverse, the iconic jug pisser man would go around town collecting pee, paying the urinators a half-a-penny a jug.

Collecting pee for the processing of wool was nothing new. This not very happy looking man was following a two-thousand-year-old profession.

Archaeologists digging in the ruins of Pompeii uncovered several examples of the above-pictured structures. From literature and other research, they determined that this site doubled as Roman laundries and Roman fulling workshops. The pits would contain rancid urine, and the motive power would be human washing machines. The cloth to be finished would be immersed in the urine and then, the fuller, holding onto the columns on each side, would trample the textile with bare feet in the same way that Italian peasants used to crush grapes for wine. Roman fullers were so skillful that they could produce woolen togas as soft and fine as silk.[17] These shops also served as Roman laundries because the same process was used to clean clothes. Working these treading stalls knee-deep in smelly pee was, not surprisingly, considered a degrading job, and fullers appear in Roman literature as objects of derision. The Roman elite may have made fun of fullers, but they depended on them because social custom dictated that they must appear in public in the most spotless of white togas. The ammonia in rancid urine was an ideal cleaning agent to remove food and grease stains deposited during those notorious all-night orgies. As chemist Joe Schwarcz explains, "A solution of ammonia in water is alkaline, and alkaline can break down fat into soluble fatty acids."[18] Then the togas would be hung over a frame below which was burning sulfur used to bleach them further. Finally, they would be rinsed in clean water to remove some of the stink. The relative whiteness of your toga was a measure of class distinction. Senators had to sport the whitest of togas, whereas lower-class citizens could wear togas of a grayer hue, ones that spent less time being stomped on in the pee.

Mention of the profession of fulling appears several times in the Bible, as in this passage from The Gospel according to Mark.

> After six days, Jesus took with him Peter, James, and John, and led them up a high mountain by themselves. There he was transfigured before them. And his raiment became shining, whiter than snow, whiter than any fuller on earth could possibly have bleached it.

The Roman poet Seneca recommended the 'fuller's leap' as a form of ancient cardio. Lucilius, governor of Sicily in AD 65, who was perhaps getting fat around the middle from all those orgies, was told to imitate the vigorous foot pounding of the fullers. Seneca told him that stomping in place, presumably sans urine, makes for an excellent workout.

Here on a fresco found in Pompeii, we see these human washing machines in action. This leads us directly to the subject of Roman tax law.

In AD 69, Emperor Titus Flavius Caesar Vespasianus Augustus – Vespasian for short, had ambitious building projects, including Rome's now iconic Colosseum. But his treasury was low on funds. Like Emperors everywhere, he looked around for something more to tax and came up with a lulu. To collect their valuable washing liquid, the fullers of Rome cleverly placed empty urns in strategic locations such as outside taverns. Patrons would obligingly fill them up. Emperor Vespasian had the brilliant idea to tax the collection of this essential commodity. When his son complained about the unpleasant origin of this new revenue, the Emperor gave him a lesson in high

finance. He held a gold coin up to his nose and asked him if he was bothered by the smell. The puzzled son said that it didn't smell of anything at all. "And yet," said the wily father, "it comes directly from the urine." From this we get a dictum which has resounded down the ages, *Pecunia non olet* – Money doesn't smell. His name also resounded down the ages by the fact that, 2000 years later, public urinals in France were named Vespasiennes.

The process of manufacturing woolen cloth did not change much from Roman times through the Middle Ages. This 13th century stained glass window in the medieval town of Semur-en-Auxois, in the Burgundy region of France, celebrates their local industry with an image of a man happily stamping away on a bolt of cloth knee deep in a bucket of pee. When water mills and later steam power became available, the cloth would be pounded with mechanical hammers, thus saving the soles of Europe's peasantry.

In England, the need for pee had become so acute that one owner of a fulling mill was forced to go around town with a horse and cart buying urine. Unlike the cheap Dutch, he paid an entire penny for a bucket of pee. Wool manufacturers became true pee sommeliers. The pee from redheads, considered particularly potent, commanded a penny and a half a bucket. One Welsh manufacturer would pay the princely sum of two pennies if the family of urine producers were Methodists. The sect abstained from drinking alcohol, so he was convinced that their urine was more concentrated. A manufacturer from England, William Partridge, had his own pee preferences. "Urine from persons living on a plain diet is stronger and better than urine from luxurious livers," he wrote. "Cider and gin drinkers produces the worst urine; beer drinkers are considered to produce the best."

In Old English, fulling, this process of shrinking and giving body to wool, is called *waulking*. Author Sally Magnisson notes that all the families with the name 'Walker' in the phone book can trace their ancestry to *waulkers*, people whose profession required extensive dips into buckets of stale pee. She interviewed traditional crafters of Harris Tweed in the far North of Scotland and found out that they prized the use of urine until well into the 20th century, long after store-bought compounds were readily available. They swore that pee worked better.[19]

The final step in the manufacture of cloth is dyeing. Here again, urine played an essential role. The main source of blue dye in the Middle Ages was a humble looking weed called woad.[20] To make dye, its leaves were fermented and dried into a powder. The cloth was then soaked in a vat of this powder mixed with urine. Urea, the main component of pee, is what is known as a mordant, coming from the Latin word to bite. A mordant bites into the fibers of the wool and the molecules of the dye and binds them together to make the color fast. Without a mordant, your blue suede shoes would be washed white in the first rain storm. If you see some blue fabric from the Middle Ages, you now know it has been soaked in pee. The other colors have faded in the magnificent 900-year-old Bayeux Tapestry pictured here, but the vibrant blues are a vivid testament to the lasting powers of this 'divine nectar.'

By the 16th century, England had become a major textile center. It had lots of sheep and skilled workers producing and exporting fine English woolens to Europe. The most effective mordant, even better than pee, is a mineral called alum (ammonium aluminum sulfate). In its natural form, it was mined in a mountain near Rome which just happened to be owned by the Vatican. When Henry VIII broke away from the Roman Catholic Church, the Pope, retaliated by cutting off England's supply of this precious mineral. The textile industry was in a panic and almost ready to collapse when, in 1600, a chemical genius discovered a way of converting gray rock shale into alum. This shale is found in great abundance in the cliffs of the northeast coast of England, in Yorkshire. The complex, many-step process required an enormous quantity of ammonia, which in this pre-industrial era could only come from stale, smelly, rancid... need I go on? Large alum producing plants, perhaps the world's first chemical factories, were established in Yorkshire, but the local supply of urine could never keep up with the demand. By some happy synergy, ships plying the coast were bringing goods from Yorkshire to London and returning with their holds empty. Given its population and its number of taverns, London was probably the largest producer of human urine in the world. Ship owners realized that they could double their income by engaging in a two-way traffic–with goods and raw material going to London, and London pee being transported back to Yorkshire. Soon barrels filled with thousands of gallons of this odorous commodity were sloshing their way north, and the British textile industry was afloat again.[21]

Because it has an ability to soften leather, pee even played a key role in the printing process. Aside from typesetting, one of the most crucial jobs in early printing was that of the so-called beater. His job was to apply ink to the type before it was pressed onto the paper. Too little ink and words or letters would be missing. Too much ink and the page would be filled with blotches. These skilled craftsmen used two soft leather inking balls to apply the ink to the type. The word 'soft' is key here. The

process would only work well with the softest of leather balls, and it was the job of the printer's apprentices to soften the leather for these balls each morning by stomping on them in buckets of urine. No wonder these ink-smeared, evil-smelling young men were called printer's devils.

When we look at the magnificent examples of pre-industrial printing from the Guttenberg Bible to Johnson's English dictionary, we now know that, if their pages were chemically analyzed, we would find more on them than the author's words. Perhaps a DNA test of those famous First Folios will finally settle the question of who was the person who wrote Shakespeare's plays.[22]

The final essential use of pee comes from the fact that the ammonia in rancid urine reacts with oxygen in the air to form nitrates. Nitrates perform two important functions for the human race; they grow our food, and they can blow us up. Pre-industrial societies made ample use of this first property. Night soil, the contents of a city's household chamber pots and outdoor privies, were regularly collected and sold to local farmers as fertilizer.

The use of pee to make explosives is more complicated. Some goofy anarchist sites give a recipe that uses urine to make a powerful explosive. Although the chemistry is correct, it is much quicker and easier to make explosives from the nitrates in commercially available fertilizers than by boiling down pots of pee. The potential explosive power of pee, however, does add a fascinating footnote to the history of the American Civil War. One of the key ingredients in gunpowder, and the most difficult to obtain, is potassium nitrate – KNO_3. This chemical, also known as saltpeter or *nitre*, is the stuff that makes gunpowder explode. It is a mineral mined in caves that had been coated with centuries of bat guano. During the American Civil War, the North had plentiful sources of this mineral, but as the war dragged on, Southern forces were running desperately short of saltpeter. No gunpowder, no war.

A Southern chemist, John Haralson, knew that potassium nitrate could be produced directly from human urine and, on October 1, 1863, he placed this announcement in the *Alabama Sentinel*:[23]

> **The ladies of Selma are respectfully requested to save their chamber lye. Barrels will be sent around to gather up the lotion.**
> John Haralson, Nitre Agent, Confederate States Army.

Chamber Lye is a polite euphemism for pee. His appeal to the ladies did not end up producing much gunpowder but, boys being boys, it made for some hilarious poetry, some of it turned into song. This from the Confederate side:

> *John Harrelson, John Harrelson,*
> *Where did you get this notion,*
> *To send your barrel around the town*
> *To gather up this lotion?*
> *We thought the girls had work enough*
> *In making shirts and kissing,*
> *But you have put the pretty dears*
> *To patriotic pissing,*

They say there is a subtle smell
That lingers in the powder;
That when the smoke grows thicker,
And the din of the battle louder
That there is found to this compound
One serious objection;
A soldier cannot sniff it
Without getting an erection.

When Union Soldiers got wind of this project, they answered with this poem of their own:

John Harrelson, John Harrelson,
We've read in song and story
How a women's tears through all the years
Have moistened fields of glory,
But never was it told before,
How, 'mid such scenes of slaughter,
Your Southern beauties dried their tears
And went to making water.

No wonder that your boys are brave,
Who couldn't be a fighter,
If every time he shot a gun,
He used his sweetheart's nitre?
And, vice-versa, what could make
A Yankee soldier sadder,
Than dodging bullets fired by
A pretty woman's bladder

FIVE
PISS PROPHETS

And now, as the Monty Python crowd was fond of saying, for something completely different. This is a chapter about how urine has been used as a diagnostic tool, but surprisingly, we begin with a fierce debate involving Federal law and civil liberties. One of the most fundamental liberties of the US Constitution is the Fourth Amendment which bars government officials from searching our homes, our person or our property without a valid legal reason. Along with freedom of speech and of religion, this is one of the foundations of American liberty. In 2002, the Supreme Court was to decide on a case that seemed to threaten this freedom.

In their zeal to pursue the so-called war on drugs, the elders of the Tecumseh, Oklahoma School District came up with an extraordinary ruling. If a student wanted to participate in *any* after-school activity, they would have to submit to a drug test. Every student who wanted to play chess or volleyball or become a cheerleader or a member of the FFA (Future Farmers of American) or the FHA (Future Homemakers of America) would have to pee in a cup.

According to the regulations posted on the School Board's website, "The specimen must be collected in a restroom or other private facility behind a closed stall. The Principal shall designate a coach, sponsor, or school employee of the same sex as the student to accompany the student to a restroom or other private facility behind a closed stall. The monitor shall be present outside the stall to listen for the normal sounds of urination in order to guard against tampered specimens and to ensure an accurate chain of custody. The monitor shall then verify the normal warmth and appearance of the specimen." [24]

This is the sort of treatment you might expect for prisoners in a high-security penitentiary, not of some shy 10-year-old girl wanting to become a 'Future Homemaker of America.' And there are more serious consequences to this blatant invasion of personal privacy. The inexpensive urine test being used by the school system is notoriously unreliable, producing 5% to 10% false positives.[25] In addition to this fact, certain common foods such as poppy seeds and over-the-counter drugs will trigger an indication that the child is abusing opioids. Taking an allergy pill, or having eaten a bagel before the test, could brand Junior as a drug abuser for the rest of his life.

Naturally, some parents objected to this testing, considering it a form of child abuse. Common sense tells us that this is a clear violation of our Fourth Amendment rights–forcing presumably innocent children to have the most intimate chemistry of their bodies examined by government-sanctioned strangers. On June 27th, 2003, the opinion of the court in 'No. 01-332, The Board of Education of Independent School District No.92 of Pottawatomie County versus Earls' was announced by Justice Clarence Thomas. Five of the nine Justices voted to deny the students their Fourth Amendment rights.[26] What is surprising about this case is that those black-robed gods who called themselves conservative and so often denounced the powers of "big government" saw fit to allow government to intrude on the privacy of innocent young children.

150 million of these drug tests are conducted in the United States each year, and no one is safe from this

invasion of pee privacy. If you want to get a job with many companies, you are required to pee in a cup. In 15 states, if you are poor and your family is applying for food stamps, you are similarly presumed guilty and have to engage in this supervised urination to prove your innocence. A few puffs of pot and your family starves. You are not even safe at home from this specter of drug testing because there is also a huge market for over-the-counter drug testing kits. "Test yourself or a loved one," is the advertising slogan for a product called *Reveal*. The company promises that the product will be sent to you in 'discreet packaging' – presumably so your 'loved one' doesn't know what is coming.

Just as the Vietnam War spawned many memorable protest songs, so this war on drugs produced its musical opposition. The Commander-in-Chief who began this war was Ronald Reagan. In 1988, Tom Paxton wrote a prophetic song; *We're Filling a Bottle for Ronnie:*

> *They're gonna be testing our children,*
> *And you can be certain of that.*
> *They're gonna be testing our old maiden aunts*
> *And they're gonna be testing our cats.*
> *They used to go looking for traitors*
> *Who commonly hid under beds,*
> *Now, 'stead of them stirrin' up all of this urine,*
> *They ought to try testing their heads!*

We're filling a bottle for Ronnie,
We're filling it up to the brim,
We'll never rest till we pass the test,
For we all think the world of him.
We're filling a bottle for Ronnie,
And we'll never kick up a fuss,
For we're only doing to that little bottle
What Ronnie's been doing to us.

These days, with the ambiguous legality of marijuana, crafty entrepreneurs have figured out a way of making money from this never-ending war. Amazon, for example, is awash in companies offering to sell synthetic pee to help one cheat this ubiquitous testing. But the anti-drug Gestapo is vigilant to the dangers of urine substitution. That is why you have the strange scene in Oklahoma of monitors with their ears to the door, not only listening to children tinkle, but also holding a thermometer at the ready to confirm that the pee is delivered at "normal warmth." And under some authorities, just listening at the door is not invasive enough–now they insist on actually watching you pee.

Enter the *Whizzinator*.

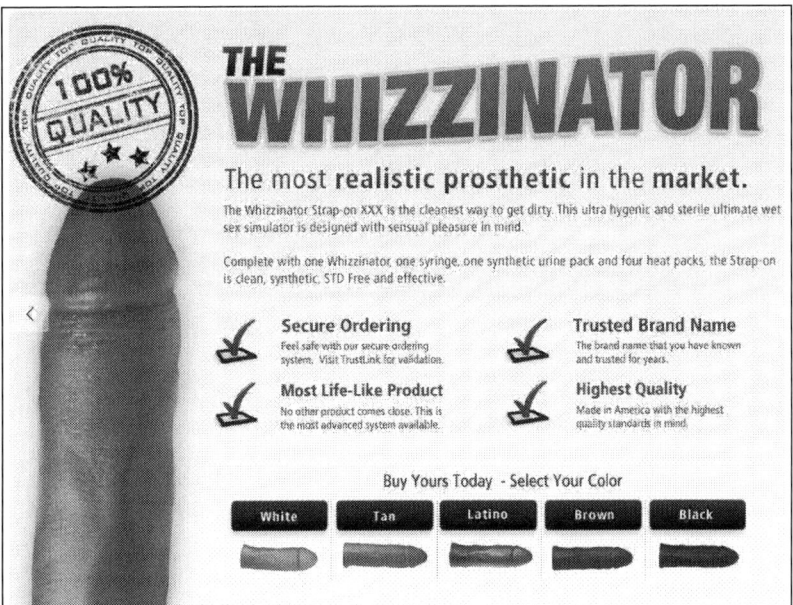

"Whizzinators.com is proud to sell the newly released model of the Whizzinator the Whizzinator Touch. This model is operated by squeezing the head of the penis from top and bottom to release the flow. Inside the head of the penis is a "pressure release valve" which opens up when you squeeze it. With every kit, you have the option of choosing between the following colors, white, tan, Latino, brown or black."

And coming out of your Latino colored penis is drug-free pee at just the right temperature because the *Whizzinator* also boasts a built-in heater.

Since woman drug takers don't have to pull anything out to perform in front of the pee inspector, some people have come up with ingenious do-it-yourself solutions to the problem. One parolee wrote in a panic to one of the many how-to-fool-a-drug-test websites and got this homely advice from a pro.

"Get yourself a lemon juice squeezer and fill it with clean urine. Stick it on up your vagina. I'd say at least for like two hours. Get yourself a piece of Mac's Ear Wax stuff. Place it over the opening. (Because you will NOT be able to unscrew the cap with one hand without looking obvious.) Have the opening about 1/3 of an inch outside of you. Sit down, hold the pee cup in place and ACT NORMAL. Slowly remove the wax with one of your fingertips, let it drop into the toilet and cough or sigh really loud while doing this. Then use your 'female' muscles to squeeze a little of the urine out to hit the toilet water and then catch the rest in a cup. You will need the stream to sound like the real thing. Then WIPE with a BIG piece of toilet paper to cover up the little clear wax that is in the bowl. BUT YOU MUST PRACTICE!!!!!!!!! A GAZILLION TIMES! if you aren't confident in this method! I can't garuntee (sic) this method, but it works for me! Most IMPORTANT thing is to PRACTICE!"[27]

Perhaps an important lesson for all of Oklahoma's Future Homemakers of America is learning how to sigh with a lemon in their vaginas.

Testing urine for drugs is so effective because, as we have learned earlier, urine is a byproduct of blood. It is an indelible marker for any chemical we are putting in our bodies.

Drug testing is headline news in the world of sports, where drugs, particularly steroids and human growth hormone (HGH), give athletes that little edge they need–often just a few milliseconds–to beat competitors over the finish line. Recently, the government of Russia has practiced drug cheating on an industrial scale. No *Whizzinator* needed here. During the 2014 Sochi Winter Olympics, Russian operatives used James Bond-like tactics, with secret panels in the walls of the testing rooms, to swap steroid-laced urine with virgin-pure pee. When discovered, it became a scandal of major proportions. After years of state-sponsored drug cheating, hundreds of Russian athletes have been retroactively stripped of their medals, and the entire country was banned from participating in future Olympics until they clean up their act. Alas, they are not the only sinners. Professional and amateurs in every sport, from bicycle racing to baseball, have been brought down by their own urine, which, as we have learned, can never tell a lie.

> For we must all appear before the judgment seat of Christ that everyone may receive the things done in his body, according to that he hath done, whether it be good or bad.   Corinthians 5

This property of urine was even more significant in a pre-industrial age when physicians had no way of knowing what was going on inside our bodies. In a world before blood tests, MRI's and X-rays, examining what came out of our bodies, particularly pee, was the most important diagnostic tool available to doctors.

This detail from a 17th-century painting shows the full extent of the doctor's diagnostic tools. He is taking the patient's pulse, and about to inspect the young girl's urine nervously held at the ready by the patient's mother. The artist Jan Steen painted several of these scenes, and the 'illness' would be readily recognized by his knowing audience as that of a lovesick teenager.

Medical theory from the time of the ancient Greeks through the 18th century believed that our health was determined by a balance of fluids in our bodies–the so-called four humors. Because imbalance meant sickness, doctors concluded that it made sense to examine carefully that most abundant fluid, the patient's urine. Dr. Ruth Harvey, at the Centre for Medieval Studies at the University of Toronto, reminds us that examining urine "was almost the only diagnostic tool available to a profession that had no firsthand experience with internal anatomy, no conception of electricity, germs or the circulation of the blood, and no instruments other than their own eyes to explore the mysteries of the human body." [28]

Much as the stethoscope became the symbol of the physician in the 19th century, the so-called jordan or bulbously shaped bottle used to examine urine was the universal symbol of medicine of a previous era.

In this illustration from Chaucer's Canterbury Tales (written in the 14th century), we have the physician immediately identifiable by what he is holding. Chaucer also reminded what doctors love the most: *"Gold in phisik is a cordial / Therefore he lovede gold in special."*

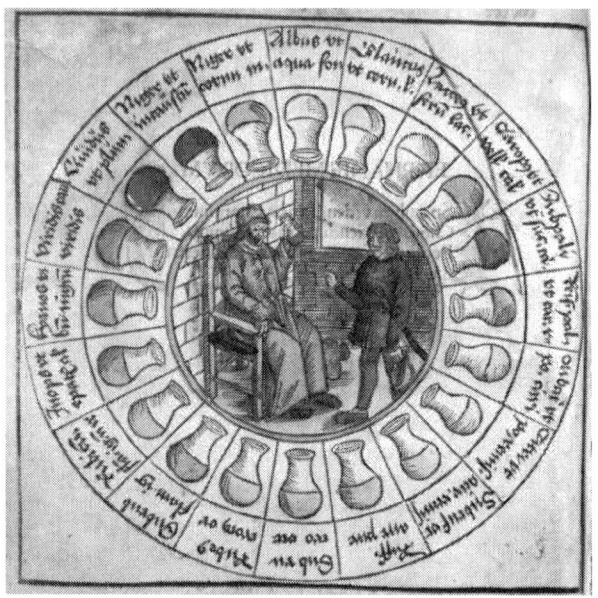

Many books and manuscripts from this period instruct doctors on the fine art of inspecting the uroscope. In a plate from an early medical book, we see the doctor examining a jordan of urine surrounded by a color wheel, each color supposedly representing a particular disease. And color was not the only property to be examined. Did the pee have bubbles or foam on top or some form of solid precipitate in the bottom of the container? The doctors carefully smelled and even tasted the urine.

Dr. Ruth Harvey explains their bizarre view of the workings of the human body.

> Urine essentially told the physician the state of the patient's digestive processes, which were charmingly described as an internal cooking process. The stomach was set above the liver like a cauldron over a fire, and the food was 'cooked' there until it was turned into the substrate of blood. The liver was in charge of the process, but if it failed to cook the food sufficiently or overdid the process and burned it, all sorts of dire internal consequences ensued. The patient's urine faithfully reported on all of them.[29]

As strange as these theories seem to us, medieval doctors did have one virtue sadly lacking in today's high-tech medicine. Doctors back then looked at the whole patient making medical practice in the Middle Ages essentially humane; medicine as an art rather than as a science.

> Every patient is slightly different, and it was very important to consider the individual circumstances as well as the wider world. Each living thing is made up of an individual blend of elements, and everyone is affected by the same elements in the world around them. A good physician must consider not just the age, sex, occupation and personal condition of the patient, but also the season of the year, the place of habitation, the prevailing wind, and the astrological environment. Man, as the most elaborate creation in the world, reflects this whole composition within himself: he is the microcosm, or little model, of the universe. The elements inside him have to be in balance for him to be healthy. Urine, as the product of a threefold digestive process, is the most informative messenger of what is going on.[30]

Some doctors saved shoe leather by omitting the visit to the patient. They had the patient's urine flasks brought to them and issued prescriptions from the comfort of their own offices. Some claimed that they could even detect a broken bone simply by examining the crystal ball of someone's urine.

By the 17th century, people were beginning to question the practice of uroscopy. In 1637, a British member of Parliament, Thomas Brian, had enough of all these pretensions and wrote a book whose title page says it all.

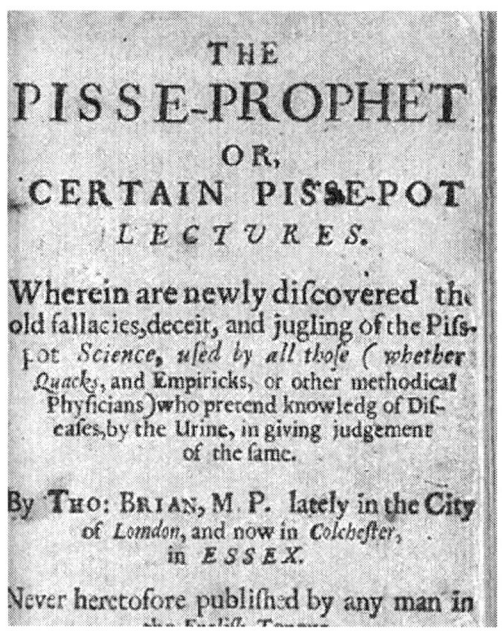

"Wherein is shew'd the errour of the common people (who thinke that Diseases are to be discerned by the Urine) and the fallacies of the Physician, who intimate the same unto them."

In spite of the growing suspicion that piss doctors were quacks (and perhaps because doctors could offer few accurate diagnoses or cures), the practice of urine examination continued for hundreds of years. In the late 18th century, a London Doctor, Theodore Myersbach, raised the art of uroscopy to new heights of absurdity. He claimed that, simply by examining pee, he could instantly tell not only the state of a person's health, but their age, their sex, and their full life story. His practice flourished, with theater celebrities and British lords and ladies either coming to his office in person or having their servants deliver a pot of their urine to be examined. Dr. Myersbach could examine up to 200 patients a day–an impressive record even for today's assembly-line medicine. In 1776, a suspicious reporter from *The Gazetter* brought him a bottle urine produced by the family horse, claiming that it was his wife's pee. After carefully examining its color and composition, Myersbach determined that the patient had a severe cough and prescribed a dose of opium. The fraud was reported in the newspaper, but it did not seem to hurt the good doctor's business or his considerable income.[31]

In truth, the color of our pee more often shows what we are eating or drinking than the result of disease. So, for those very special occasions in your life, here are some recipes for Technicolor pee: For red pee, eat a plate full of beets or rhubarb, for bright orange pee, down a gallon of carrot juice. To produce a toilet bowl of spring green, eat lots of asparagus. But if on its own your pee suddenly turns blue, purple, or brown, I would recommend a quick trip to the emergency room.

The modern piss prophet is your doctor's laboratory. Here your little cup of pee undergoes a rigorous chemical analysis. What is, or is not, in the urine will help diagnose a range of conditions, including kidney disorders, liver problems, or a urinary tract infection which is very common in women. For men, we have the PSA (prostate-specific antigen) tests for prostate cancer, a major killer. Recently, this test has become controversial because a positive test can result in one of the more unpleasant procedures of modern medicine–a prostate biopsy. "This is going to be a little uncomfortable," says the doctor as he inserts a large needle up your penis. A 2014 study demonstrates that trained dogs could diagnose active prostate cancer with 97% accuracy simply by sniffing the sample of urine.[32] The fact that doctors still resort to the painful needle rather than using a canine assistant shows that, even in this so-called scientific age, doctors may be more concerned with appearances – the theater of medicine – than unorthodox procedures that might really work.

The art of uroscopy was not a complete fraud because, long before the 20th century, competent doctors could actually diagnose some major illnesses by examining a patient's urine–the most significant being diabetes.

Diabetes was known as 'the pissing evil' because of its most obvious symptom, the need to urinate frequently. A description of the disease is found in an Egyptian papyrus dated 1552 BC. Only in the 20th century researchers discovered that one of the causes of the disease was a lack of insulin, a hormone produced by the pancreas which enables the body to metabolize sugar. Without insulin, we pee out unabsorbed glucose. The disease was easily diagnosed by early doctors who would routinely taste the patient's urine. Its official Latin medical name *diabetes mellitus* describes the symptoms of the disease—*diabetes* from the Greek *diabainein*, which means liquid passing directly through you as in a funnel, and *mellitus*, Latin for sweet as honey.

In modern times, the standup comedian Patrice O'Neal announced to the world that his girlfriend had diagnosed his diabetes long before his doctor suspected that he had the disease. He went on to explain that she enjoyed his golden showers (much more about that subject in a later chapter) and one day she reported that his pee had begun to taste sweet, like birthday cake.

The most famous and spectacular victim of a urinary catastrophe was King George III of Great Brittan. In 1788, the poor monarch not only had to deal with the aftermath of losing America but suddenly and ominously his pee turned a dark red. He began having convulsions and then would rip off his clothes and run around the palace completely naked. Declared insane, he was tied to a chair until these symptoms and his urine came back to normal.

Modern doctors have diagnosed his problem as a rare metabolic hereditary disease called *porphyria*. George recovered, but then relapsed in 1811, once more with a change in the color of his urine. The job of ruling was taken over by his eldest son whose morals were scandalous but whose urine was an acceptable hue. Poor George. Despite his bad press in America, he really was a very good king. He died blind and demented in 1820. [33]

Blind, demented, urine-challenged King George III in old age.

George III was not the only porphyria-ridden monarch in European history. Vlad III of Romania, third son of Vlad Dracul was also known as Vlad the Impaler because his favorite method of executing his enemies was to impale them on a stake. He too was said to have suffered from acute *porphyria*. Apart from madness, one of the other symptoms of *porphyria* is an extreme sensitivity to bright light. This fact may form the basis of the myth that vampires were allergic to sunlight, coming out only at night to drink the blood of their victims. Vlad also had dark red urine, a fact only helping to enhance the original Count Dracula's sanguine reputation.[34]

The medieval concept that links the color of urine to most diseases is absurd, but one thing that the color of pee will measure with great accuracy is your level of hydration. The less water you drink, the darker yellow is your pee. That is the explanation for a 21st century urine color chart. Tom Herman, the head coach of the Texas Longhorn football team, noticed that his young players were not drinking enough while playing hard under the broiling Texas sun. For all athletes, dehydration is a dangerous, potentially deadly condition. Coach Herman decided to make the copious guzzling of water an indicator of team spirit. He posted this chart in his players' bathroom shaming them into achieving 'champion level' pee coloration. It worked wonderfully, and Herman's pee posters are now to be found in locker rooms around the country. [35]

The other major piss prophesy that has lasted the ages is the test for pregnancy. At least thirteen centuries before Christ, doctors knew that there was a unique substance that appeared in a woman's urine soon after she became pregnant. A papyrus described a test in which a woman would urinate on wheat and barley seeds over the course of several days. If the seeds sprouted, this was a sign that she was pregnant. Testing this theory in 1963, scientists found that indeed, the urine of pregnant women did promote the seeds to grow 70% of the time, while the urine of non-pregnant women did not. We now know that the seeds sprouted because of the presence in the woman's urine of human chorionic gonadotropin (hCG), a hormone secreted by the placenta after the fertilized egg is implanted in the uterus.

This test was forgotten, and the following 3000 years were truly the dark ages for pregnancy testing. From the time of Christ well into the 20th century, folk medicine had all sort of wacky procedures thought to indicate pregnancy. One involved placing an onion in a woman's vagina at night; if she didn't have onion breath in the morning, she was declared pregnant. In Iceland, they put a sewing needle at the bottom of a bowl of the woman's urine. If the needle rusted, it was thought to show that she was pregnant. One scholar, Albert Magnus, in his book *Secreta mulierum et virorum* (Secrets of Men and Women, 1493), tells us to give a suspected pregnant woman a sweet drink before she goes to bed. If she complains of a pain in her navel in the morning, pregnancy is confirmed. Magnus warns that it is important not to tell the woman the purpose of the drink because women are very sneaky.

Only in the last century did scientists discover a real link between pee and pregnancy. In 1927, two German researchers, Bernhard Zondek and Selmar Aschheim, developed a test for the hormone hCG by injecting a woman's urine into a female rabbit. If the rabbit ovulated, the message went back that it was time to start putting money into the college fund. In television shows, when a character runs into the room with the cry, "The rabbit died!" you would know that our heroine was going to have a baby. Unfortunately for the bunnies, in truth, every rabbit had to be killed and cut open to see if it was ovulating. Until a chemical test for the hormone hCG was invented in the 1960s, millions of rabbits were sacrificed on the altar of piss prophecy. For anxious men and women, the experience of taking what had become known as the A-Z test (after the initials of its inventors) was a stressful experience. It meant the expense and inconvenience of a trip to the doctor, a whiz in the cup, and an agonized wait of several weeks for the results of the test.

Not surprisingly it was a woman, Margaret Crane, who put an end to all this rigmarole and changed the world of piss prophecy and women's lives forever. A freelance designer, she had been hired by the pharmaceutical company *Organon* to work on a new line of cosmetics. While touring the company's laboratory, she saw the research being conducted on a chemical test for that telltale hormone hCG. At her home in New York, she assembled a plastic paper clip holder, a mirror, a test tube, and an eyedropper, and developed the world's first home pregnancy test kit. "I thought how simple that was," she recalled, "a woman will be now able to do that herself." [36] Not so fast Margie. Vigorously defending the most cherished tradition of the medical profession since the time of the ancient Romans–the right of doctors to make lots of money—one physician in an editorial published in *The American Journal of Public Health* raged against the use of these home tests, urging that they be made illegal.

By the 1970s, however, the sexual revolution was in full swing and women were determined to take control of what was happening in their own bodies. Ms. Crane's creation appeared on drug stores shelves under the very predictable brand name, *The Predictor.*

Soon many brands of inexpensive kits were on the market. Today, any woman can take the test in the privacy of her own bathroom. An indicator line on the tiny screen shows her the future of her race, and millions of rabbits around the world will live to tell the tale.

SIX
PHOSPHORUS

It is 1669. We are in a dark, evil-smelling basement laboratory in the city of Hamburg. For weeks, Hennig Brand had been boiling down vat after vat of rancid human urine–1500 gallons in all–until it was reduced to a grayish paste. Oblivious to the almost overpowering stench, he then heated this paste at a high temperature and, using apparatus that would be familiar to a modern chemist, he passed this vapor through cold water. As Brand watched in absolute astonishment, something miraculous began to happen. The waxy liquid dripping through the water began to light up the dark room with an eerie green light and then, spontaneously, it burst into flame. Wildly elated, he was convinced that he had captured a prize that had eluded researchers for centuries. In this glowing mass of boiled pee, Hennig Brand thought he had discovered the secret of the universe. He called the substance *phosphorus mirabilis*—the miraculous bearer of light.

Hennig Brand was not a chemist but an alchemist, a  discipline that was part science, part magic, part religion, and part fantasy. Its theory and workings are very difficult for a modern person to understand. We can study the ancient books on the subject and stare at their intricate drawings and complex formulae and still not have any idea of what it all means.

Their laboratories looked scientific, with beakers, retorts and an array of powders and liquids—indeed, many alchemists were skilled chemists—but their mental world was radically different from our own. Like the urine-examining physicians in the previous chapter, they had a holistic view of reality in which heaven and the movement of the planets and stars were directly linked to everything that happens here on earth, including what goes on inside our bodies. Fully understand this link, and you gain universal knowledge and infinite power.

The main goal of alchemists, one for which they would toil entire lifetimes in dark, smoke-filled laboratories, was to convert an ordinary metal, generally lead, into gold. Today we know this was an impossibility, but the prospect of creating infinite wealth through chemistry was very real to thousands of very smart people from the Middle Ages through the 18th century. Sir Isaac Newton, one of the greatest scientific minds in history, practiced alchemy, as did many of the founders of modern chemistry. And why not? They had the evidence of their own experience that boiling, burning, melting, or dissolving something in acid could radically transform one substance into another having very different properties. Liquids could become solid; red powders could become black; solids could explode into gasses. So why, with the right mixture of this and that, heated to just the right temperature, using just the right container, could they not transform lead or anything else into gold?

Kings and emperors sponsored resident alchemists who, like today's cold fusion energy researchers, promised that infinite wealth was just one or two experiments around the corner. Some were charlatans who would conceal small bits of gold in the bottom of their retorts, and make them wondrously appear at the right moment. But most alchemists believed in what they were doing, although, by the very nature of their work, they were extremely secretive. Their alchemy books are filled with secret codes and mystical symbols making them beautiful to look at, and impossible to decipher.

 Hennig Brand's life work was not being sponsored by any ruling monarch. He got his funding the old-fashioned way—by marrying wealthy women. A pompous man who insisted on being called Herr Doktor Brand, he obtained a large dowry from his first wife and ran through her money pursuing his passion for alchemy. When she died, (Are we to imagine from the fumes coming from the basement?) he married an even richer woman whose gold allowed him to carry on his elusive search for even more gold.

All of this does not explain why the Herr Doktor was boiling down vats of urine, or why he was so excited when he produced this glowing bit of goo. Brand, like other alchemists, believed that gold was present in all matter and his task was to refine this matter into the perfect purity that lay hidden within. Alchemists had a mystical belief that they were striving not only for the metal gold but also a magical liquid, a universal medicine–the elixir of life. What better substance to start with, Brand reasoned, that the golden liquid coming out of human beings themselves. In refining this raw material, pee, he had discovered a substance that not only miraculously glowed forever, but would spontaneously burst into fire. He was sure that the paste he had captured in his retort was nothing less than the essence of life itself.

Today we know that Brand actually did make an amazing discovery–the element phosphorus. But the knowledge of this fact, and even of the existence of chemical elements, would only be understood several centuries later. True to its pee origins, phosphorus was assigned the chemical symbol 'P,' while poor potassium, a far more common element, was left to make do with the confusing symbol 'K.'

As the possessor of the elixir of life, Brand was understandably paranoid about his discovery. He kept it secret for many years, but inevitably his recipe for turning urine into phosphorus–how can I resist this one–leaked out. In the next century, it was discovered that phosphorus also could be derived from ground-up bones. It was soon manufactured on an industrial scale in a process that no longer needed vats of stinking pee. But Brand's discovery of phosphorous led to a wonderful new invention–matches, a most useful product in a world that was heated and lit by fire. So, in a very real sense, the element did live up to its name, *phosphorus mirabilis*–the miraculous bearer of light.

SEVEN
PISSOIRS

On September 20, 2001, the musical *Urinetown* premiered at Broadway's Henry Miller Theater. The timing couldn't be worse. It was barely a week after the attacks on the World Trade Center, and an ominous black cloud of smoke still hung over the city. As the title suggests, the musical was an exercise in pure silliness. The plot involves an evil corporation getting control of the city's dwindling water supply and enforcing a ban on all private toilets. In this urinary dystopia, everyone was required to pay to pee. Music numbers included songs such as *It's a Privilege to Pee*, and *Run, Freedom, Run*. In the scene when the corporation is overthrown, and people are once again free to pee whenever and wherever they want, the cast sings, *I See a River*.

It turned out that this musical absurdity was just the escapism that New York needed.[37] The play won three Tony Awards, ran for almost one thousand performances on Broadway, and has been touring and in continual revival ever since. A silly story, but it touched on a very real dilemma expressed in the full bladders of men and women in all the major cities of this country–where to pee.

In pre-modern, less fastidious times where to pee was not at all a problem. Drawings and literary references all make it clear that the ancients peed anywhere and anytime they felt the need. To understand how this was possible, we have to appreciate that pre-industrial sanitary engineering was almost non-existent. If a time machine were to transport us back to any large city before the mid-19th century, the first thing we would notice would be a horrible smell. For example, the streets of ancient Rome were piled high with garbage and human and animal waste of all kinds. Photographs show that the situation was not much better in New York City only 150 years ago. Dead horses would fester in the streets until ultimately disposed of by marauding dogs and rats. It was said that, if the wind was blowing in the right direction, you could smell New York City on a ship six miles out to sea. In medieval cities and 19th century London, residential buildings were jammed next to slaughterhouses, tanneries, and as we have seen, very malodorous laundries. The London summer of 1858 was called 'The Great Stink' because all the sewage and industrial waste flowing untreated into the Thames River was festering in the heat. Only then did Parliament, its windows sealed against the unbearably foul odors, vote money to upgrade the city's sewage system.[38]

Ancient Rome's much-celebrated sewage system carried off mainly rain water; the waste from public and private toilets just overflowed onto the streets. Most people did not have toilets but used chamber pots, which they emptied out the nearest window along with any household garbage. As the Roman poet Juvenal tells us with only slight exaggeration, being drenched with human excrement was the least of your worries:

> You may well be deemed a fool, improvident of sudden accident, if you go out to dinner without having first made your will, for there is death in every open window as you pass under at night. You can hope, and put up a piteous prayer in your heart, that the residents may be content to pour down on you *only* the contents of their slop-pails!

In this 2000-year cacophony of smells, a little pool of urine on the street or up against a wall would be the least of the era's olfactory and sanitary problems. Edinburgh, its population concentrated in multistory tenements, was singled out as a particularly foul place. Until modern times its nickname was the evocative Auld Reekie. Tobias Smollett in his 18th century novel *Humphry Clinker* accurately describes the scene and the smell.

> Every story is a complete house, occupied by a separate family, and the stair being common to them all, is generally left in a very filthy condition. A man must tread with great circumspection to get safe housed with unpolluted shoes. Nothing can form a stronger contrast, than the difference betwixt the outside and inside of the door, for the good-women of this metropolis are remarkably nice in the propriety of their apartments, as if they were resolved to transfer the imputation from the individual to the

public. You are no stranger to their method of discharging all their impurities from their windows, at a certain hour of the night, as the custom is in Spain, Portugal, and some parts of France and Italy. A practice to which I can by no means be reconciled; for notwithstanding all the care that is taken by their scavengers to remove this nuisance every morning by break of day, enough still remains to offend the eyes, as well as other organs of those whom use has not hardened against all delicacy of sensation.

Even the splendors of the palace of Versailles were flavored with human excrement, as described in a letter written by a sister-in-law of Louis XIV.

> There is one dirty thing at Court that I shall never get used to, the people stationed in the galleries in front of our rooms piss and shit into all the corners. It is impossible to leave one's apartments without seeing somebody pissing. [39]

In the 19th century, Lord Byron was banned from Long's Hotel on London's Bond Street for constantly using a corner of the foyer rather than bothering to go down to the basement latrines. And then there was this notice posted in a London gentleman's club:

During the asparagus season, members are kindly requested not to relieve themselves in the hat stand.

This warning notice brings up a fascinating bit of pee trivia. Asparagus, because it contains certain sulfur compounds, gives people's urine a distinctive smell described variously as like rotten cabbage by many people, and like a flask of perfume by the eccentric French author Marcel Proust. Although everybody excretes asparagus pee soon after eating the vegetable, the fascinating fact is that only one-third of the human race have the particular gene that allows them to detect any smell at all.

At home, until the relatively recent advent of flush toilets, most people peed into chamber pots or somewhere near a chamber pot, as demonstrated in this 1814 drawing of a typical English dinner party. Servants would later empty full chamber pots often out the nearest window.

If the dumper were polite, he or she would first call out *'gardez l'eau!'* (French for 'watch out for the water!'), from which it is believed that the British derived both the word 'loo' for bathroom and the necessity of wearing wide-brimmed hats when walking down the street.

Chamber pots are nothing new. This Greek one from around 480 BC pictures an image of a prostitute peeing, perhaps to inspire the user.

Later centuries saw very elegant pieces of china. They could be found under the bed or hidden in a discreet piece of furniture.

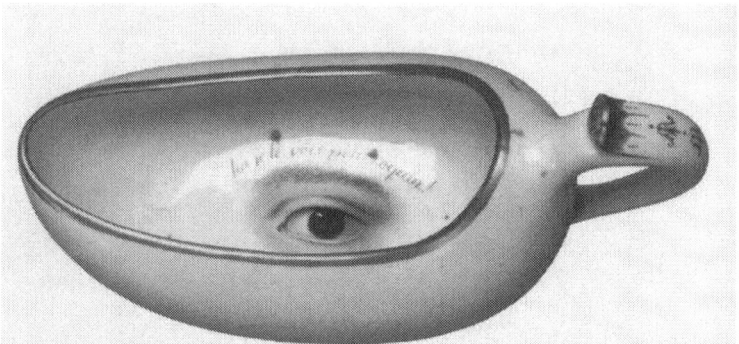

There were bathroom humor chamber pots.

And utilitarian chamber pots like this one.

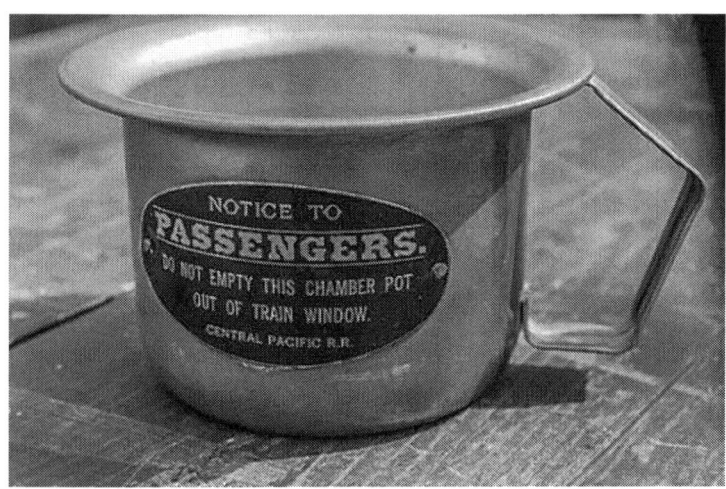

Some chamber pots even made a political statement. This rare antique below features a picture of Benjamin Franklin Butler, the brutal Union general who occupied the City of New Orleans after the Civil War. He had no trouble getting the men of the city to submit to federal authority, but the women were not so ready to give in. On May 26, 1862, he passed General Order No. 28, commonly known as the infamous 'Woman Order' which, in effect, gave the occupying Union troops the right to rape any local woman who showed them disrespect. The ladies of the city responded to the order by using this chamber pot with the portrait of 'Beast Butler' and then emptying the contents of the pot on the head of any unfortunate Union soldier who happened to be passing under their window.[40]

Women in a previous age wore long dresses but no panties, so they had no trouble using these handy items when the need arose. Here is very the moment captured by the 18th century painter François Boucher. The young lady is adept at peeing while not wetting her fine petticoats or elegant dress.

The most curious type of chamber pots used in the 18th and 19th centuries was a portable version called a *Bourdaloue*. This device was named after a French Jesuit preacher, Louis Bourdaloue.[41]

It was said that Father Bourdaloue's sermons were so lengthy but so fascinating that the ladies did not want to miss one word. So, while still sitting in church, they would deftly slip the above-named device under their skirts and do their business still taking in every gem of his divine wisdom. The vessel was oblong or oval in shape with a slightly raised lip at one end and a handle at the other. The edges curved inward to avoid hurting the woman's tender parts. Tin-glazed or porcelain, they were decorated with flowers or painted scenes. Many were gilded. Today they are to be found in antique stores eagerly purchased by collectors who use them on elegant dinner tables as gravy boats.

The reign of the chamber pot did not really end until the 20th century when plumbing and toilets came into general use. But public toilets were considered a real novelty and, as we have seen at the beginning of this chapter, in many cities, they still are.

In 1851, visitors flocked to the Crystal Palace in central London. They marveled at the huge glass and steel building, the exhibits from countries around the world, and the steam turbines and the telegraph. The exhibition space also had public washrooms featuring something most Londoners had never seen before–flush toilets. Visitors would first pay one penny to an attendant, enter the toilet stall, do their business, pull the chain, and thrill to the flush. Almost a million visitors visited these wonders of the age; soon 'spending a penny'

became the specifically British euphemism for our own euphemism—going to the bathroom.[42]

Paris introduced public urinals as early as the 1830s, and by the 1930s there were well over 1000 of these slightly odorous conveniences on the main streets of the city of lights. Named *Vespasiennes*, you will remember, after the pee-taxing Roman Emperor, they were simple affairs, barely hiding the urinary actions of the exclusively gentlemen urinators. These humble appliances fascinated American visitors and somehow contributed to the thrilling reputation of the French for moral looseness. The author Henry Miller waxes poetical about them in his novel *Black Spring*.

> When I touch the subject of toilets, I relive some of my best moments. Standing in the urinal at Boulogne, with the hill of St. Cloud to the right of me, and the woman in the window above me, and the sun beating down on the still river water. I am passing on this quiet knowledge to other Americans

who will follow me, who will stand in full sunlight in some charming corner of France and ease their full bladders.[43]

Some people did more than just ease their bladders. The American sociologist Laud Humphreys described what he called 'the tearoom trade'– anonymous, highly risky homosexual encounters in this virtually public space.

Tourists could not get enough of the novelty of being able to pee freely near a busy sidewalk. I have a shaky home movie of my late father emerging smiling from a Paris pissoir in the 1950s. Feminism, modernity, and perhaps overly sensitive noses doomed these green wonders in the 1980s. Pictured here is the last *Vespasienne* in Paris, a preserved, interactive piece of French history, still wafting the odor of a bygone age.

The disappearance of the once ubiquitous pissoirs had a very predictable consequence. Parisian men have resumed pissing on the nearest wall or lamp post. The problem is particularly acute around bistros and commuter train stations. Said one railway official, "People going home from a night out are relieving themselves before they get on the train. It smells bad and costs a fortune to clean. And the neighbors are complaining."[44]

Laurent Lebot and Victor Massip came up with a 21st century solution. They call it the *Uritrottoir*. (Trottoir is the French word for sidewalk.)

Looking like planters, and placed in strategic locations, the units are filled with dry straw or sawdust.

CIVILIZEZ LES PIPIS !

They are high-tech; each urinal is equipped with an electronic monitoring system that transmits a signal when the straw or sawdust has become completely soaked. The contents are then picked up by workers and transformed into compost for the city's parks and gardens. Parisian pipi, at least from men, has truly become civilized.

Meanwhile back in the new world, nothing much has changed. Public facilities are still rarities, and Americans continue to perfume walls, back alleys, and subway platforms. A teacher of mine at Boston University had a basement apartment near a tavern. He spent weary nights in vain attempts to ward off patrons watering his windows. Some cities have opted for high-tech solutions. San Francisco engineered a wall curved in such a way that when you peed on it, it would splatter the liquid back onto your pants. The Metropolitan Atlanta City Rapid Transit Authority, MARTA, is spending millions of dollars to install electronic urine detection devices in all its elevators. When someone pees inside an elevator, a strobe light will flash, a siren will sound, and the alarm will trigger a call to MARTA police, all before the startled offender even has a chance to zip up his fly.[45]

For years, New York City has also attempted to mitigate its pee problem. It put out contracts for elaborate pay toilets that would be large enough for the handicapped, but that somehow would not become a base for drug addicts and the homeless. The project failed spectacularly. But there are a few public facilities, including this one costing $250,000 in a park near Times Square. It features not only safety and cleanliness but fresh flowers every day.[46]

Poorer countries do not have this problem. In the absence of public facilities, private entrepreneurs operate toilets costing the equivalent of several cents to use. Because of low wages, they are able to be staffed by willing employees who keep these facilities clean and safe. The result; people do not pee on streets, and their subways and underpasses are sweet smelling. This sign advertising such an operation in Mexico City graphically dramatizes its purpose.

Unlike ancient Rome with its communal, multi-holed places of defecation, modern humanity prefers to pee and poop behind closed doors. The one curious exception to this rule is the public urinal. These consist of a series of receptacles, sometimes separated with the skimpiest suggestion of a partition, or sometimes, with no partitions at all. Certain venues, particularly sports stadiums, offer urinal troughs. Like a bunch of farm animals, troops of men are expected to pour their steaming, beer-propelled torrents into these communal pots.

Social convention dictates that you stare at the tile wall not at your neighbor or his member. Many men find the practice of public peeing a little too public and hey furtively scurry into a toilet stall pretending they have a more serious operation to perform. About 10% of American men report that they have difficulty urinating in the presence of others. This condition, like everything else in life, has an official medical name: *paruresis*, also known as "Shy Bladder Syndrome," or "Ballpark bladder."

There is a human instinct to create art. In the hands of innovative designers, the humble urinal becomes a canvas for unlimited creativity

Peeing into a urinal is a learned experience. A company called *Babyyuga* sells a practice urinal for use at home so that, while turning the froggy's windmill, the young pisher prepares to aim for greater things.

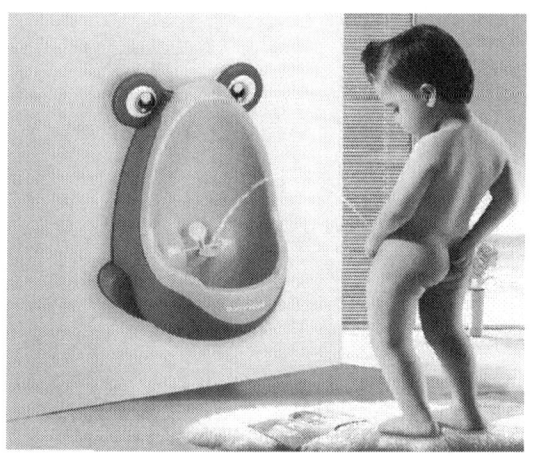

If female readers are getting urinal envy from all these images, have no fear, capitalism is here. Manufacturers offer a variety of products allowing women to pee standing up. They are called Female Urinary Devices–FUDs, for short.

And why, apart from surprising men at a urinal, would a woman want to pee standing up? Manufacturers of FUDs list many reasons including long car rides, traffic jams, traveling, music festivals, bicycle trips, climbing, skiing, dirty toilets, armed forces, sailing, kayaking, canoeing, and fishing. And during camping trips, a woman standing to pee avoids the danger of some insect crawling up her derriere as she squats in the bushes.

FUDs are also said to be useful for the mobility impaired and policewomen on the go.

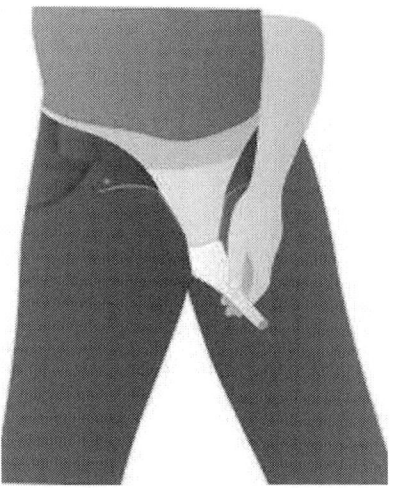

One brand, The *Shewee,* (now at a new low, low price of only $10.50 plus shipping & handling.), is a plastic funnel device promoted as washable and reusable. Its ad line: *"Stand up and take control!"* *Gogirl* markets a similar device with the ad line *"Don't take life sitting down."*

All this is well and good for the pee-ers on terra firma, but what about those pissers on the move? Along with having told you about the gallons of urine in swimming pools, I am now about to reveal another fact that you probably would prefer not to know. Super hydrated NFL football players have perfected the "slow release" technique of peeing in their pants.[47] Marathon runners and bicycle racers, knowing that every second counts, also do not stop to pee. "It took two years of fairly messy trial and error," said runner Ryan Sandes, "but I finally mastered 'the art of the sneaky pee.' The trick is to properly gauge wind directions. A real pro will never make the mistake of pissing into the wind." [48]

Other athletes on the move are golfers. Imagine this scene: you are surrounded by friends, drinking, putting, and having a grand old time when suddenly at the fourth hole, you really, really have to pee, and there is not a tree or bush is in sight. Fear not because you own a *UroClub*™.

The UroClub™ is the discrete, sanitary way for your urgent relief. Created by a Board-Certified Urologist, it looks like an ordinary golf club but contains a reservoir built into the grip to relieve yourself. The *UroClub*™ is leak-proof, easy to clean. No more embarrassing moments.

When you see how the makers allow you to pee into a golf club inconspicuously, you have to admire the inventive genius of America. The hollow club comes with what is advertised as "a privacy shield," a green cloth that hooks onto your belt and, according to the manufacturer, frees both hands so that you can manipulate the club, your zipper and your penis. I would imagine this may take long periods of training. A *Uroclub* pro must learn to disguise those furtive hand movements under the green cloth while, at the same time, he must avoid watering his expensive golf shoes.

Another group of people in motion are the truckers zooming down the long highways of America. They pee in large water jugs and toss them out the window. In many states, thousands of these never-disintegrating bottles of pee line the highways and are creating a huge mess.[49] Cleanup crews working the roadside ditches call them urine bombs because the bottles actually explode when hit by their lawnmowers, soaking the operators with rancid pee. Fines of up to $1000 have little effect because time is money for truckers, and rest stops are an infrequent option.

The last group of moving pee-ers to be dealt with in this chapter are, at this very moment, careening around the earth at 17,150 miles an hour. The occupants of the International Space Station also have to pee and, for a multitude of reasons, tossing bottles of urine out the window is not an option. The sixty-year history of peeing in outer space begins with a very simple method–they didn't. In the beginning, spaceflights were so short that astronauts were just told to hold it in. For slightly longer flights, space age diapers were invented with a gel that could contain large amounts of pee. Later, the

Space Shuttles were furnished with very advanced toilets because nobody wanted weightless pee or worse floating around the cabin. The toilet, which astronauts nicknamed 'Mr. Thirsty,' consisted of a plastic funnel connected to a tube under suction.

Our intrepid explorers would place the cup-shaped funnel to their member and let go. For once in their lives, women had an easier time peeing than men because, if not carefully manipulated, the male astronaut's penis could get lodged in the ever-sucking tube, and–Houston, we have a problem–his foreskin could be launched into outer space.

Peeing while weightless did have its moments of special pleasure. Columbia Astronaut Story Musgrave used to urinate upside down. Also, when vented into the near-absolute-zero temperature of outer space, the pee would instantly crystallize into an icy cloud of starry flakes having an iridescent sparkle of extraordinary beauty. Astronaut Wally Schirra liked to call it 'Constellation Urion.'

With its large crews and many-month voyages, the designers of the International Space Station knew that they could no longer support these uranic light shows. Because urine is 95% sterile water, they were able to turn this liability into an advantage by connecting their toilets to a wildly intricate recycling contraption. Here it is, with NASA's wildly complex description of its operation:

"This is a close-up view of ECLSS Water Recovery System (WRS) racks. The MSFC's ECLSS Group oversees much of the development of the hardware that will allow a constant supply of clean water for four to six crewmembers aboard the ISS. The WRS provides clean water through the reclamation of wastewaters, including water obtained from the Space Shuttle's crew member urine. The WRS is comprised of a Urine Processor Assembly (UPA), and a Water Processor Assembly (WPA). The UPA accepts and processes pretreated crewmember urine to allow it to be processed along with other wastewaters in the WPA, which removes free gas, organic, and nonorganic constituents before the water goes through a series of multi-filtration beds for further purification. Product water quality is monitored primarily through conductivity measurements. Unacceptable water is sent back through the WPA for reprocessing. Clean water is then sent to a storage tank." [50]

This acronym-laden description cannot conceal a simple fact. Like the yogis of old, all 21st century astronauts now drink their own pee.

EIGHT
PLEASURE & PERVERSION

Havelock Ellis (1859-1939). *The Unrecognized loveliness of the world.*

A British physician and a pioneer in the study of human sexuality, Havelock Ellis confessed that for many years he was impotent. However, one thing did sexually excite him, "I may be regarded as a pioneer," he writes in his autobiography, "in the recognition of the beauty of the natural act in women when carried out in the erect attitude. This interest was never for me vulgar but rather an idea, a part of the unrecognized loveliness of the world. This form of sexual attraction is not uncommon; it has been noted in men of high intellectual distinction." [51] I suspect Doctor Ellis included himself and his elegant whiskers in this latter category.

Ellis, psychoanalyzing himself, attributes his excitement at watching women pee to his close relationship with his mother. His father, a sea captain, was absent for long periods during which time he enjoyed a closeness with his mother. He would sponge her back in the tub and, as a twelve-year-old prepubescent, would watch her urinate. Whatever its root cause, Ellis is correct in saying that this particular fetish is common, although exact statistics are difficult to obtain. One small survey reports that twenty-five percent of couples have done it at least once, but this must be compared with sixty-two percent saying they used feathers or fur during sex, and ninety-three percent of those interviewed saying that they have enjoyed the occasional spanking.[52]

Urolagnia: noun, def. Sexual excitement in associated with the sight or thought of urine or urination. From Greek ouron - urine, & lagneia - lust.

Given the enormous variety of things that excite people sexually, from rubber face masks to tennis shoes, it is hardly surprising that urine and lust should form an easy marriage. Sex and urine live in the same neighborhoods and, in males at least, they use the same apparatus. In addition to this fact, all of us feel mild pleasure when emptying a full bladder. Psychiatrists after Ellis have had a field day with the subject, throwing around Latin and Greek words to impress us with their wisdom. They have variously labeled the fetish urophagia, renifleurism, undinism, and ondinisme. And further nuancing the subject, a pee-pleasure authority, Doctor R. Denson, writes that the term 'undinism with urophagia' should only be used when "fetishism leads to oral incorporation of the urine." Doctor Denson also specifies that urination may serve sadistic (peeing on your partner) or masochistic (being peed upon) purposes and therefore these acts should be labeled 'urosadism' and 'uromasochism' respectively.[53]

The object of all this verbal foreplay is to give an official diagnosis to the patient who admits to this pleasure, using a code number found in the *Diagnostic and Statistical Manual of Mental Disorders* (the DSM). Doctors need this code number to get paid. "Urosadism and uromasochism are erotic foci," the manual explains, "suggesting that in some cases urophilia would fit more appropriately under part 2 of criterion A in DSM-IV and DSM-IV-TR, which refers to a focus on suffering and humiliation of oneself or one's partner." [54] As we thumb through the fine print of this one-thousand-page tome, we might suspect that the so-called science of psychiatry is nearer to the piss prophets of medieval times that its authors would like to acknowledge.

You don't have to believe in psychoanalysis to realize that adults who engage in urolagnia are often re-enacting scenes from their childhood. An early loss of innocence comes at that time of life when we are first told that we that we can't pee whenever or wherever we want to. In most cultures, inappropriate urination will result in a whack to the behind, an event that will surely continue to resonate in the deep recesses of our collective minds. But Freud had an even wackier explanation for the fetish: [55]

> 1) Humanity's most important act was the taming of fire.
> 2) Fire signifies desire and the penis.
> 3) There is a primal desire in all males to extinguish fire using the stream of their urine.
> 4) Women cannot stream their urine.
> 5) Therefore, men get pleasure and dominance from this power.

Away from the world of psychiatry, people call this sexual practice 'water sports' or 'golden showers' (and most people use fire extinguishers to tame fire.) Boldface names who admit to indulging in urine lust include the pop star Rick Martin and the actor Andy Milonakis, who shocked People Magazine by confessing in an interview that he liked the feeling of "warm urine" on his chest during sexual intercourse. Frank Zappa would sing in the chorus of Bobby Brown Goes Down: "I can take about an hour on the tower of power/ Long as I gets a little golden shower." Annie Sprinkle, an American porn actress, performance artist, and an advocate for female sexual enjoyment, chose her stage name from her obsession with pee. More about her later.[56]

Finally, if we are to believe a report by a British spy, it seems that even President Donald Trump participated in this liquid pleasure with prostitutes in a Moscow hotel room. He later insisted that this could never have happened because he is germophobic. Vladimir Putin supported his denial while at the same time patriotically praising the versatility of Russian call girls.[57]

For our history of the subject, we must inevitably turn to the twisted mind of that sewer human depravity, Donatien Alphonse François, otherwise known as the Marquis de Sade. A raving sexual maniac who practiced what his now famous name denotes, he was imprisoned in the Bastille. There, on paper smuggled into the prison and glued into a forty-foot roll, he wrote, in tiny print, what he considered his masterpiece; *Les 120 Journées de Sodome ou l'école du libertinage* (The 120 Days of Sodom, or the School of Sexual Indulgence).

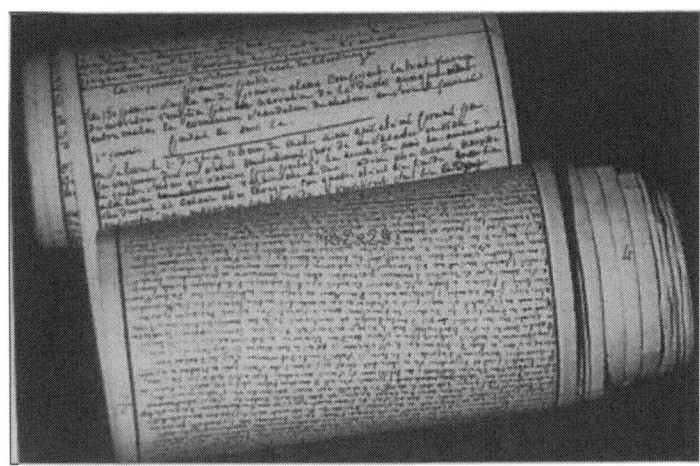

The history of this document is worthy of a Hollywood thriller. Hidden behind the walls of the prison, the manuscript was later discovered, and in the 1990s it was the subject of a lengthy legal battle by descendants of de Sade and various other parties claiming ownership. Ultimately the scroll sold for almost ten million dollars, and it is now on display at a private museum in Paris. Reading its stream of consciousness list of horrors, one regrets that the document was not burned by the mob storming the Bastille. Its urolagnia fantasies are among the most benign – at least they do not involve torture or mutilation – but they still make difficult reading even in our jaded Internet era with its cornucopia of perversions.

What follows is Sade's imagined scene between an aging priest and a young girl who has previously been given several glasses of juice to drink:

> He asked me if I felt like peeing. I told that I had a powerful urge to do so but was embarrassed to satisfy myself in front of him. "Oh my god you must, my little scamp. You must do it not only in front of me but <u>on</u> me."
>
> He then pulled his prick out from his breeches and said, "Here's the tool you're going to inundate." Whereupon he lifted me up and set me down between two chairs, one foot on one chair, the other foot on the other. He then spread the chairs and told me to squat. Holding me in this posture, he placed a vase underneath me. His prick was in his hands right under my cunt. Kissing me, he said, "Off you go, my little one, water my life with your warm, enchanting

outpouring. It will be the empire of all my senses. Piss, dear heart, piss away!"

The sweetest ecstasy came as the liquid from my swollen stomach gushed out in abundance. The moment was crowned when we filled the vase together, he with his cum, and me with my urine.[58]

After a brief stay in a mental institution, the Marquis de Sade went on to become a minor player in the French Revolution when he was elected to the National Assembly. He eventually had a falling out with the radicals, not because of his unusual sexual proclivities, but because he objected to their cruelty during the Reign of Terror. In 1793, he was again imprisoned, this time for the sin of being too moderate.

Moderation is not what you find in the modern Internet world of pee enthusiasts. Put on your raincoat, go to the hashtag 'urolagnia' on Twitter, and stand back. You will be drowned in a vast underworld inhabited by those who pee and those who are peed upon. Some urophiliacs exult in wearing and smelling diapers, while another subset specializes in urophagia (i.e., drinking the urine). For urophiliacs, drinking urine is particularly exciting when someone pees directly into their mouth. This act is not to be confused with the spiritual/therapeutic imbibing described in a previous chapter which, although it promises eternal life, is presumably not nearly as much fun. There is a cascade of pee dating sites such as www.peemybaby.com where "people can find partners with a fetish for urination and will have a channel to vent their hidden desires." And *Kwink*, which promises to find you aficionados of the golden shower school in your local community.

There is also a wonderfully informative instructional site for prostitutes called *An Escort's Guide to Water Sports.*[59] It was written to remind sex workers that, "you never know when one of your clients will want to venture out of his standard comfort zone." The how-to instructions are extremely specific, describing many possible variations on the theme. They are given wonderfully evocative names such as *'Watering the Oak Tree,' 'Fountain of Venus,'* and the unforgettable *'Cataracts of the Nile.'*

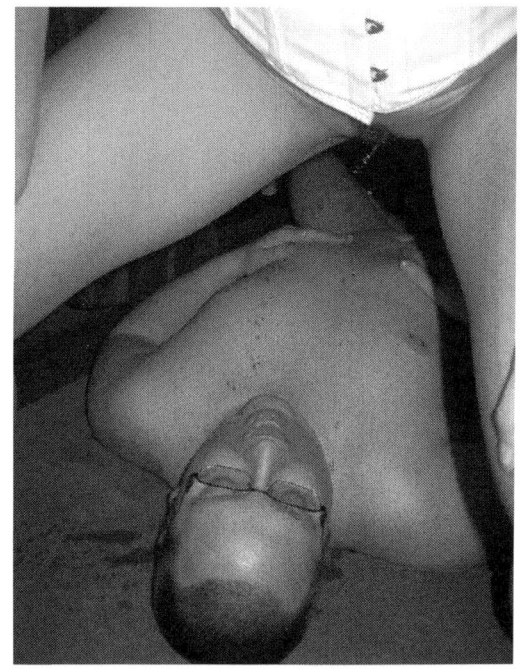

The writer of the site also provides sensible tips of a *Good Housekeeping* variety, such as, "carefully select where you will be engaging in the activity so you can avoid extra laundry." The ladies are reminded not to forget to hydrate themselves before the encounter. The real pro will even do everything to improve the taste of her urine by avoiding eating "asparagus, onions, tuna, broccoli, cauliflower, chili peppers and foods with cumin or saffron." Instead, she should consume soft drinks with artificial sweeteners which, as the attentive reader will remember from the swimming pool experiments in chapter two, pass directly through the body and so will produce sweet-tasting urine. Finally, the site gives this important piece of assurance: "It's common to have stage fright the first couple of times you engage in this activity. As you're about to let loose, turn on the faucet taps to let the water flow in the sink. Think of babbling brooks, raging rivers or wild rapids with a waterfall."

If you are finding this entire discussion a mite creepy, I can now add that immortal line from the TV pitchmen, "But wait, there's more!" And for that 'more' we now visit that island of bizarre sexual creepiness, Japan. There is a distinct infantilism in Japanese male sexual fanaticizes–witness the abundant imagery of school girls in short skirts. But when it comes to the specific Japanese version of urolagnia, I believe that they deserve whatever golden statues are given out for weirdness.

They call it. Omorashi (おもらし / オモラシ / お漏らし), sometimes abbreviated as simply "Omo." The literal translation of お漏らし is 'leaking.' Apparently, some Japanese citizens experience sexual arousal from seeing someone dancing around with a full bladder or, even better, someone wetting themselves. There are Omo Facebook pages, a very active Twitter hashtag, Omo blogs, and www.omorishi.org where enthusiasts are invited to share pants-wetting literature, drawings, photographs and YouTube videos of people dribbling all the way to the bathroom.

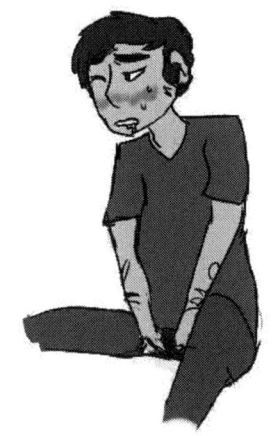

The blogger Stephen Alexander defines this fetish with great precision.

"It should be noted that for most devotees of Omorashi, an exchange of bodily fluids is not desired; they neither wish to piss on others nor be pissed on by them. Nor do they want to see naked organs in close-up action, or hope that things might develop in an overtly sexual manner. For the obsession is ultimately with clothed incontinence and Omorashi videos tend to focus on the garments worn by the participants; these invariably include schoolgirl uniforms, but films with women dressed as business professionals–looking dignified and in control, before shamefully succumbing to the need to urinate–are also very popular with certain male viewers." [60]

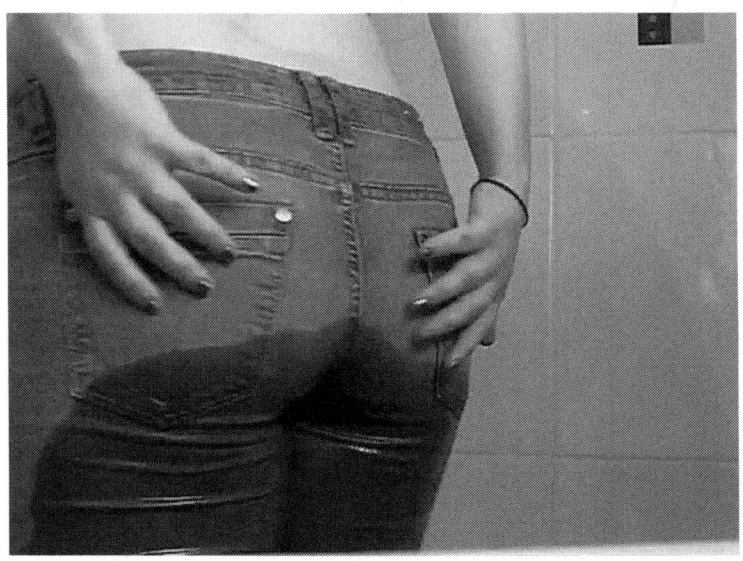

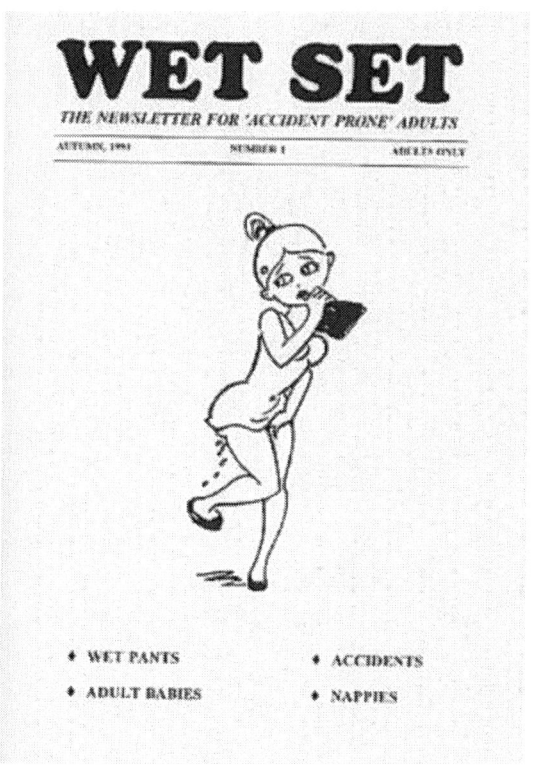

In Australia, *Wet Set* is a newsletter for "accident prone adults," also featuring "diaper lover and other urolagnia related material." [61] In their *Dripping Wet Magazine*, the publishers promise readers 'pisstasy' as they flip through its full-color pictorial section featuring "Glita marking out the way with a golden trail" and "Nikki's private messy moments." From this and the profusion of Omo websites, it is clear that, like other Japanese cultural innovations such as sushi bars and manga graphic novels, Omorashi has become an International passion.

NINE
PISS ART

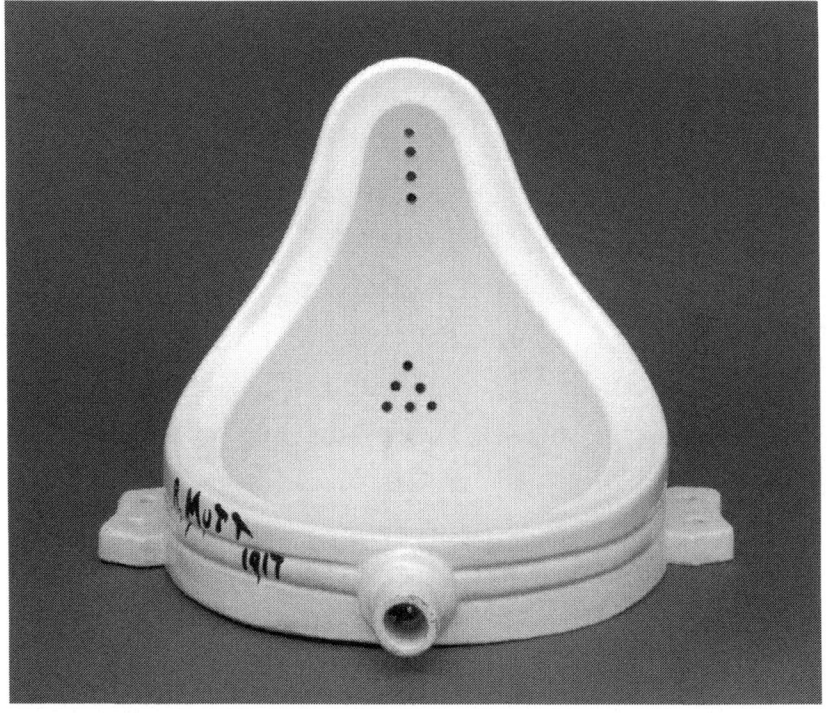

During the last 100 years, the object of many artists has been to *épaté la bourgeoisie* (to shock the bourgeoisie). This practice can be considered, on the one hand, a bit childish, and on the other hand, lots of fun. The medium that many artists use and continue to use to do this shocking is excrement or something connected with excrement.

A pioneer in what we may call this excremental movement is that Dadaist genius, Marcel Duchamp. In 1917, the Society of Independent Artists was staging their first annual exhibit in New York. Duchamp, proving that he could out avant-garde even the most daring of artists, bought a urinal from the J.L. Mott Iron Works company, turned it upside down, and signed it "R. Mutt, 1917." The bourgeoisie running the show were so shocked that they rejected his 'work of art,' thus launching his fame and the most continually annoying question of the modern era, "What is art?" Tragically, the original urinal which British critics have voted as "the most influential artwork of the 20th century," was tossed into the garbage, but the work has survived in many reproductions produced by Duchamp. One such signed urinal sold at Sotheby's auction house for $1.7 million.

Attempting to shock the shocker, on August 25, 1993, the performance artist Pierre Pinoncelli approached one of these replica urinals on exhibit in a museum in France, pulled down his pants, and peed into it. This desecrator of this fine art was arrested, of course.

Following the dictum that, "everything changes except the avant-garde," the idea of using pee to shock or amuse was being used by writers and artists long before there even was a bourgeoisie. Here, from 100 BC, is a statue of a very drunk Hercules showing that even Greek demigods need to pee.

Chaucer, writing in *The Canterbury Tales* in the 1380s, has the wife of Bath describing poor, long-suffering Socrates having to deal with his shrewish wife, Xantippe. Note that he uses the once perfectly respectable English word, 'piss.'

No thyng forgat she the penaunce and wo	Nor did she forget the pain and sorrow,
That Socrates hadde with hise wyves two,	That Socrates had with his two wives,
How Xantippa caste pisse upon his heed.	How (when) Xantippe threw piss on his head.
This sely man sat stille as he were deed;	This silly man sat as still as if he were dead;
He wiped his heed, namoore dorste he seyn	He wiped his head but didn't say anything more,
But, "Er that thonder stynte, comth a reyn."	Than "Once the thunder's over, then comes the rain."

A couple of hundred years later, Shakespeare in *Twelfth Night* has the buffoon Malvolio falling for a forged letter and saying that he recognizes the woman's handwriting while the character inadvertently makes this rollicking pun:

> MALVOLIO: By my life, this is my lady's hand. These be her very **C**'s, her **U**'s, **n**' her **T**'s, and thus makes she her great **P**'s.

In the same era in France, François Rabelais was having similar fun in his bawdy tale about the father and son giants, Gargantua and Pantagruel. In this chapter, Gargantua is sitting atop Notre Dame Cathedral in Paris, annoyed by the huge crowd below making an enormous fuss about him. Laughing he said,

> "Just for that, I'll now give them some of their wine." He then untied his pants and drawing his penis out into the open air, he so pissed on them that he drowned sixty thousand four hundred and eighteen people... Some escaped this piss-flood by running away and, when they were on higher ground, they began to swear and curse, some in anger some with laughter (*les unes en colere, les autres par ris*). Ever since the city has been called par ris–Paris.[62]

It is probably from Rabelais that Jonathan Swift got the idea for his own giant pissing scene in *Gulliver's Travels*. The book was written in the 18th century not as a children's tale but as a biting political satire. The scene was cut from the book in the prudish 19th and early 20th centuries. It is a pity because most children I know would have thoroughly enjoyed this part of the story.

Several of the emperor's court, making their way through the crowd, entreated me to come immediately to the palace, where her imperial majesty's apartment was on fire, by the carelessness of a maid of honor, who fell asleep while she was reading a romance. I got up in an instant; and orders being given to clear the way before me, there being a full moon, I made sure to get to the palace, without trampling on any of the people. I found they had already applied ladders to the walls of the apartment and were well provided with buckets, but the water was at some distance. These buckets were about the size of a large thimble and the flame was so violent that they did little good. The case seemed wholly desperate and deplorable, and this magnificent palace would have infallibly been burnt down to the ground, if, by a presence of mind unusual to me, I had not suddenly thought of an expedient. I had the evening before drank plenty fully of a most delicious wine called Glimigrim which is very diuretic. By the luckiest chance in the world, I had not discharged myself of any part of it. The heat I had contracted by coming very near the flames, and by labouring to quench them, made the wine begin to operate on my urine; which I voided in such a quantity, and applied so well to the proper places, that in three minutes the fire was wholly extinguished, and the rest of that noble pile, which had cost so many ages in erecting, was preserved from destruction.[63]

The princess, far from being grateful to Gulliver for saving her castle, was furious and swore revenge. This story is Swift's jab at England's Queen Anne, who disliked his satires, considering them vulgar. She was instrumental in blocking his ambition to become a bishop in the Anglican Church.

For visual representations of peeing, we need only look to that remarkable period in the history of painting and drawing, the Dutch Golden age of the 17th century. During this period, the tiny country of Holland dominated world trade, and a growing middle class became immensely wealthy and demanded depictions of themselves and their own lives. Up to this time, religious or mythological scenes had been the main subjects of art. Now commonplace domestic scenes would become a focus of paintings and drawings. With superb technical skill and a delicate feeling for the play of light and shadow, the world's greatest artists give us a window into the past, including the ordinary messiness of everyday life. A servant pouring milk and a woman sweeping her stoop, a family meal with the floor (as it must have been) littered with the droppings of food, a drunken scene in a tavern with a prostitute ready to ply her trade. With the low cost and wide availability of copper etchings, everyone could afford to have a print of these familiar scenes hanging in their houses.

Part of the messiness of real life is the fact that people would casually urinate in the corner of the room during a card game or a drinking session in a tavern. These artists had no desire to shock or scold. Like today's cinéma vérité filmmakers, they were simply capturing the moment. Often the results of these moments of captured reality are surreal, as in this drawing of a woman fish seller confronting a dreamy beggar in a market at night.

The greatest genius in this age of geniuses, Rembrandt van Rijn, also applied his extraordinary artistry to this most familiar of subjects.

The twentieth and twenty-first centuries are awash in every imaginable form of piss art.

David Černý, the bad boy of the Czech art world, created these two pissing men who stand at the entrance of the Kafka museum in Prague. In the country that gave us the word 'robot,' the hips of these two pee-ers swivel back and forth, and their penises move up and down. They stand in a pool of yellow water in the shape of the Czech Republic, and their penal movements are controlled by a computer. Careful observers will notice that their pee is tracing out the words of famous Prague writers on the water. Visitors are encouraged to send their own SMS text messages to these two robots whereupon they can watch their very own words being written in virtual pee. (I would urge readers to go to a YouTube site to see them in action because Černý's animatrons are a wonderful example of Czech humor and ingenuity.[64])

Never one to miss a trend, Andy Warhol joined the movement with what he called his oxidation paintings. Warhol coated canvases with copper paint, and then he would pee on them. Compounds in his urine would react with the copper to produce a series of vivid blue and green splotches and dribbles on the canvas. Although Warhol developed this technique using his own pee, he subsequently would leave the copper canvases lying around his studio and encourage his associates to be creative. His prime pee-er ended up being a gentleman who took the professional name of Victor Hugo, a pun on the fact that his penis was huge-o.[65] Not only was Victor well-endowed, but he possessed an equally large bladder.

The paintings were extremely well received when they were exhibited in Europe in 1981, lauded by one enthusiastic critic as "Warhol at his purest." Even though all these later piss paintings no longer were produced by the hand of the master, they have only increased in value over time, one selling at a recent Christie's auction for two million dollars.[66]

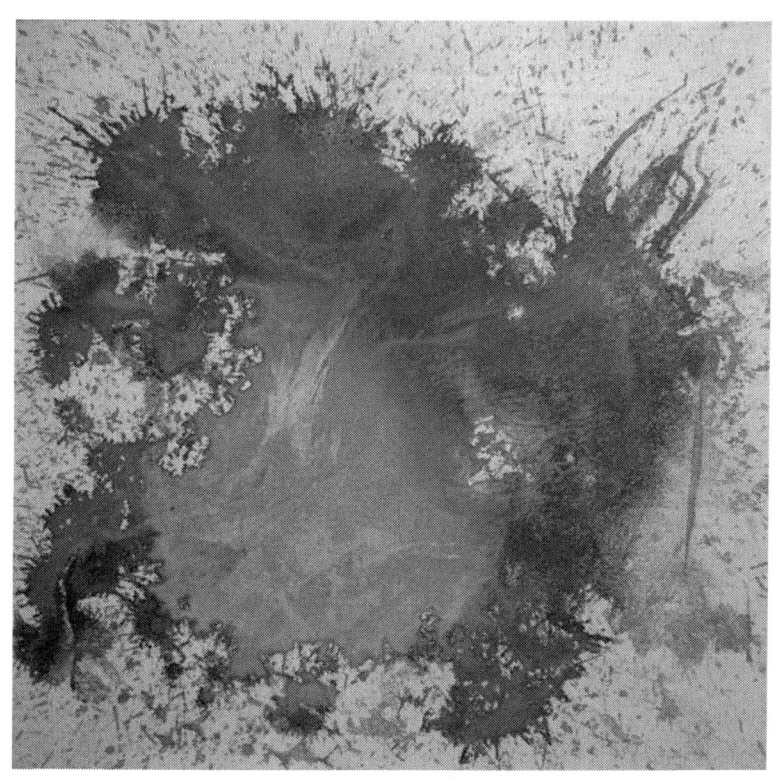

Andy Warhol *Oxidation*, copper metallic pigment and urine on canvas, 1978

The former prostitute and now performance artist Ellen Steinberg adopted the stage name, Annie Sprinkle, saying, "I love waterfalls, urine, vaginal fluids, sweat, and anything wet." One of her celebrated performances was to urinate on stage in front of a large, cheering audience.

The Canadian choreographer Marie Chouinard began her career in a similarly liquid fashion. In 1980, the twenty-five-year-old walked onto the stage of the Art Gallery of Ontario in a long white dress, drank a glass of water, and from a deep knee bend in ballet's second position, she peed into an amplified aluminum bucket. The sound of the cascade resonated throughout the auditorium. She called her performance, *'Petite danse sans nom.'* This was a petite too much for the staid bourgeoisie of Toronto, and she was banned from ever performing at the art gallery again. Peeing was the least of her transgressions. In *'Danseuse-performeuse cherche amoreux or amoreuse pour la nuit du 1er juin'* (Dance-Performer Seeks Male or Female Lover for the Night of June 1), she succeeded in pushing the envelope of performance art right out the door by auctioning her body off to the highest bidder in the audience. One critic wrote in this classic understatement that her "mold-shattering works placed her outside usual social expectations or esthetic norms." [67]

In a recent newspaper article, Chouinard denied that her object was to shock. "I am interested in contemplation. How come matter exists? Why do you and I exist? These things are a permanent mystery. As time goes by, we go deeper and deeper into these things. Also, the littlest things are endlessly fascinating. You're thirsty, and you drink a glass of water. I'm still in awe at the beauty of that."[68]

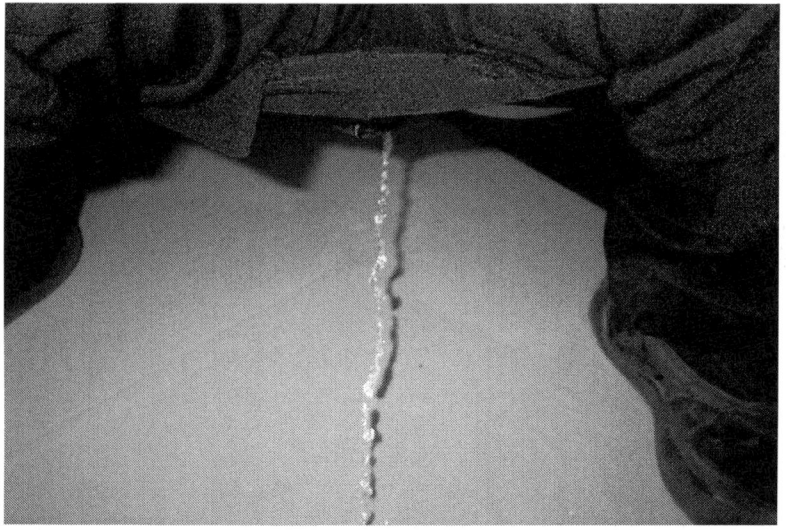

New York artist Ellen Jong is similarly in awe of beauty in her photography book entitled, *Pees on Earth*. The book consists of a series of selfies of Jong peeing around the world. According to the book's blurb, "Jong's photographs assert her place on the planet and, because we all share the act, they assert ours too. It is a manifesto for our collective existence, a cry for all sentient beings:
I am! I pee!" [69]

Now we must move from these gentle scenes of urinary beauty to a more disturbing hardcore product of the art world. In 1987, the American artist Andres Serrano peed in a glass tank, submerged a 13-inch plastic crucifix in the liquid and took a photograph of the results. It was part of a series of artworks he called *Immersions*.

Exhibited at the Stux Gallery in New York, *Piss Christ* received praise as being "formally sublime." Art critic Lucy Lippard tells us to ignore the pee and focus on "how the plastic crucifix becomes virtually monumental as it floats, photographically enlarged, in a deep rosy glow that is both ominous and glorious."

Except in the rarefied world of Greenwich Village art lovers, the work was hardly noticed or commented on. The photograph would probably have continued to be immersed in total obscurity if it had remained in New York. As part of a traveling exhibition, the crucifix photo traveled south to the home of the Bible Belt where the piss hit the fan. Reverend Donald E. Wildmon of the American Family Association now had an excellent fund-raising cause. "I would never, ever have dreamed that I would live to see such demeaning disrespect and desecration of Christ," he wrote in a mass-mailed call-to-arms. "Maybe, before the physical persecution of Christians begins, we will gain the courage to stand against such bigotry."

When it was discovered that Serrano had received a small sum of money from the National Endowment for the Art (the NEA), a taxpayer-funded agency, Members of Congress jumped into the fray. The budget of the NEA is one hundredth of one percent of Federal discretionary spending, costing every American about 50 cents a year. Most of that money goes to keeping alive small museums and art programs in rural areas across the country. But when there is political hay to be made, politicians become highly principled about government spending, and Serrano had given them a whole barnyard of outrage to work with. In memos, speeches, and newspaper articles, political leaders denounced the piece as a desecration of religion, blasphemy, odious trash, and an object designed to destroy Western civilization.

In his own version of performance art, Republican Senator Alphonse D'Amato stood in Congress and theatrically tore up a copy of the exhibition catalog containing *Piss Christ*. Republican Jesse Helms, the born-again Baptist senator from North Carolina, outdid himself in dramatic eloquence, booming from the Senate floor.[70] "I do not know Mr. Andres Serrano, and I hope I never meet him. Because he is not an artist, he is a jerk. Let him be a jerk on his own time and with his own resources. Do not dishonor our Lord."

Words became actions when Congress voted to cut the NEA's minuscule budget by an additional $45,000 specifically because of this piece by Serrano and an NEA grant awarded to the baddest boy of the American art world, Robert Mapplethorpe. Mapplethorpe had exhibited, among other outrages, photographs of a man urinating into the open mouth of another man—a triptych no less. Because of these two works, the bourgeoisie was well and truly épated, with the result that the Endowment for the Arts has been under continuous attack ever since. The Trump administration is determined to defund it completely.[71] Such is the power of pee.

Such is also the power of pee that a 32 by 42-inch photograph of *Piss Christ* "signed, titled, dated 1987 and numbered 7/10 on the reverse, in the artist's frame" sold at a recent Sotheby's auction for almost $185,000.[72] Mapplethorpe photographs now sell for more than the entire budget of the NEA.[73] Mysterious are the ways of the Lord.

Among the unmoneyed and unwashed masses, anger against *Piss Christ* only increased over time. In 2011, the photograph was on display in a museum in Avignon, France. On Palm Sunday, four people in sunglasses, aged between 18 and 25, entered the exhibition just after it opened at 11am. One took a hammer out of his sock and threatened the guards with it. In the ensuing melee, one of the group managed to take a hammer to the plexiglass screen and slash the photograph with an icepick. They also smashed another Serrano photograph, a lovely close-up of the hands of a praying nun.

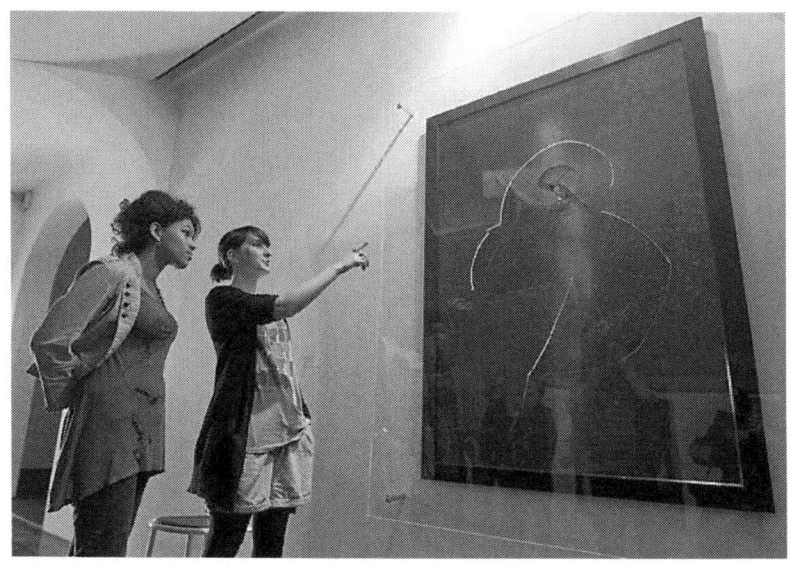

The gallery director, Eric Mézil, reopened the exhibit with the mutilated works on display "so people can see what barbarians can do." In Australia and Sweden, Catholic fundamentalists and neo-

Nazis vandalized other Serrano exhibitions. Mézil characterized these attacks on the artwork as a modern version of the Inquisition.[74]

In a recent article, Andres Serrano continued to defend his work. "For me, *Piss Christ* was an act of devotion. I was born and raised a Catholic and have been a Christian all my life. As a child and especially as I was preparing for my Holy Communion and confirmation, I often heard the nuns speak reverentially of the 'body and blood of Christ.' They also said that it was wrong to idolize representations of Christ since these were only representations and not holy objects themselves. My work was, in part, a comment on that paradox. I am neither a blasphemer nor 'anti-Christian,' as some have called me, and I stand by my work as an artist and as a Christian. Where the photograph has ignited spirited debate, that has been a good thing. Perhaps it reminds some people to question what we unthinkingly fetishize (and thereby often minimize) in lieu of pondering seriously what the crucifix actually symbolizes: the unimaginably torturous death of Christ, the Son of God." [75]

Agreeing with Serrano, the New York Times art critic Michael Brenson wrote, "How can anyone find in his work obscenity and disrespect? It is hard to believe that anyone whose faith is searching and secure would not be grateful for what Mr. Serrano has done." [76]

Really? What world do they live in? To expect people to be rational about religion ignores both history and human nature. For over two thousand years, people been fighting wars over how religious figures and symbols are to be represented. The Iconoclasts in Byzantine Turkey went around scratching the eyes out of depictions of Christ, quoting the Bible's very specific injunction: "Thou shalt not make unto thee any graven image or any likeness of anything that is in heaven above." Muslims today certainly take this edict very seriously. We are not dealing here with an academic discussion about the nature of symbols but a continuing war between and within religions with the result that real people are really being killed.

But Serrano and Brenson's greatest naivety comes not only from their innocence about religious symbolism, but from their seeming blindness to the symbolism of piss. The works of art detailed in this chapter will never give a final answer to that formerly mentioned perennial, 'What is art?' But they do and continue to deal, at a profound level, with the ultimate question of this book: what are the deeper meanings of pee and peeing?

Jorge J. E. Gracia, a philosophy professor at the State University of New York at Buffalo, discussed this in connection with Serrano's work.

> The act of pissing has important connotations that have to do with power. More in the case of men, whose act is a kind of challenge. It involves holding

your penis and pointing it outward, exhibiting the most private part of the male body, and doing it without qualms. Just showing off. Here I have something powerful, a symbol of my machismo. Let me show it to you, the proof of my virility and power as a man... The act, when done in public, becomes a sign of defiance. And when the piss is directed toward someone or something, it says: 'Hey, see, I do it on you because you are of the same quality as the piss. You are disposable, worthless, like piss.' To piss on someone is to humiliate him or her, to crush the ego, to put him or her in the proper place, a subservient place, a place of inferiority. [77]

The 18th century artist William Hogarth captures this moment of ultimate humiliation with a young boy peeing on the foot of a man imprisoned in the stocks.

As we have seen in the previous chapter, and in Robert Mapplethorpe's photographs, humiliation is precisely what gives pleasure to both the sadist and the masochist. But as Professor Gracia noted, urinating can also be an act of supreme contempt and defiance.

And here, at some anonymous protest, a very brave, if foolhardy young demonstrator shows his contempt for the police. There are no pictures of what happened next, but I hope he had a good health care plan.

But of all the images in this book, I find a blurry snapshot of General George Patton to be the most extraordinary.

In 1945, the General had been battling the Nazis, the Italians, and the Vichy French for two years. One hundred and thirty thousand of his soldiers had been killed, tens of thousands of tanks and trucks destroyed, and his reputation as a military leader was in question. On March 24, his army finally crossed the Rhine and with victory in sight the General did, what, in anguish and defeat he had been promising for years. "I drove to the Rhine River and on the pontoon bridge. I stopped in the middle to take a piss and then picked up some dirt on the far side in emulation of William the Conqueror." [78]

Primitive, childish, atavistic, but ultimately what could be a more potent symbol of victory? This moment of celebration over, Patton immediately got back to business by telegraphing the Supreme Allied Commander, General Eisenhower, "I have just pissed into the Rhine River. For God's sake, send more gasoline."

Peeing is a message of defiance and contempt, but also, as in the above example, the act demonstrates an even more primal instinct. Along with cats and dogs and deer, we humans are innately territorial and can also make the statement, "Here I've peed, so this spot is mine."

Chapter six of this book examined alchemy, the art of turning something worthless into gold. I believe that the artists and writers shown here have also performed a version of alchemy. In their work, they have taken something that we do not think much about, that we regard as the waste product of our bodies, and transformed it into a form of philosophical and aesthetic gold. (Some artists such as Warhol and Serrano, have even transmuted their pee into actual monetary gold.) In words and pictures, they show us that urine–that familiar and often reviled liquid–can tell us all something about our taboos, our fears, our deepest instincts, and our fondest hopes.

TEN
POSTSCRIPT

A personal note. When I attempted to tell friends and associates about the subject of this book, I would get a smirk, a silly pun, and then an expression of disbelief. The idea that I was seriously researching the history of pee was treated as a big joke. Writing this book is an attempt to prove my dear friends wrong.

Demonstrating that urine was the first industrial chemical, for example, gives us a powerful illustration that the past was not only a different time but a profoundly different world. Before our age of mass production and advanced chemistry, every object and every substance had value. People did not have to be told to recycle. For Victorians and before, a bit of torn cloth, used tea leaves, and coal ashes could, and would be repurposed. Even so, I was surprised to learn that urine was such an essential resource in this pre-industrial age.

Learning about early practices of sanitation was also an eye opener. The streets of cities used to be piled high with human and animal waste. Even in tidy Holland, men would casually pee in the corner of a room when they felt the need. We can only imagine what the past smelt like, and also how foreign to previous generations would be our modern notions of germs and cleanliness.

The story of uroscopy gives us a graphic window into the strange theories that early doctors had about the workings of the human body. But I was also struck by how recently the hormones found in pee were discovered and then were used in a variety of important medical procedures. Only a few generations before us, our great grandparents lived in a world without pregnancy tests, fertility drugs, and little understanding of diabetes.

In the hands of artists, pee became a medium of protest, forcing people to rethink their ideas about what is taboo. I had the same reaction in seeing how sexual practices involving pee, once considered a symptom of mental illness, are now openly celebrated around the world.

I am not going to pretend that I didn't find some of the things that I uncovered in my research very odd, but even some of these absurdities were strangely enlightening. In the end, in answer to my smirking friends, I hope I have proved that this subject is no joke, and that we all can learn many things about our past and our present by looking deeply into what, at first, might seem to be a frivolous area of study. As Senator Al Franken so aptly put it, "It's what gets me out of bed in the morning."

BIBLIOGRAPHY

Joseph S. Alter, *Gandhi's Body: sex, diet, and the politics of nationalism,* Philadelphia: University of Pennsylvania Press, 2000.

John W. Armstrong, *The Water of Life: A Treatise on Urine Therapy,* London: Ebury Publishing, 2005

Ronald H. Blumer, *Wiped: The Curious History of Toilet Paper.* New York: Middlemarch Media Press, 2013.

John Gregory Bourke, *Scatologic Rites of All Nations*, Washington, D.C.: W.H. Lowdermilk & Co., 1891.

Denson, R. (1982). Undinism: the fetishization of urine. *Canadian Journal of Psychiatry. 27*(4), 336.

John Emsley *The 13th element: the sordid tale of murder, fire, and phosphorus,* New York: John Wiley & Sons, 2000.

Miko Flohr, *The World of the Fullo: Work, Economy, and Society in Roman Italy*, Oxford Scholarship Online, 2013.

Adam Hart-Davis and Emily Troscianko, *Taking the Piss: A Potted History of Pee.* Stroud, Gloucestershire, UK: The Chalford Press, 2006.

Ellen Jong & Annie Sprinkle, *Pees on Earth*, New York: PowerHouse Books, 2006.

Sally Magnusson, *Life of Pee: The Story of How Urine Got Everywhere.* London: Aurum Press Limited, 2010.

Henry Miller, *Black Spring.* New York: Grove Press, Inc., 1963.

NASA/Marshall Space Flight Center, Environmental Control and Life Support Systems Testing Facility at MSFC, MSFC, 2001 https://archive.org/details/MSFC-0101378

Roy Porter, *Quacks - Fakers & Charlatans in Medicine*, Stroud, Gloucestershire, UK: Tempus, 2003

Lawrence M. Principe, *The secrets of alchemy*, Chicago: University of Chicago Press, 2013.

Francois Rabelais, *Gargantua and Pantagruel.* Many editions.

C. S. Rayudu, *Drink Urine and Live Healthy*, New Delhi: GenNext Publication, 2016

Paul Spinrad, *The RE/Search Guide to Bodily Fluids.* San Francisco, CA: RE-Search Publications, 1994.

Carol Steinfeld, *Liquid Gold: The Lore and Logic of Using Urine to Grow Plants*, Sheffield, VT.: Green Frigate Books, 2007

Jonathan Swift, *Gulliver's Travels*, Mineola, NY: Dover Publications, 2012

NOTES

1 Al Franken, *Giant of the Senate*, New York: Hachette, 2017, 197

2 Brad Smith, *The Oregonian*, June 16, 2011

3 http://www.ch.ic.ac.uk/rzepa/mim/environmental/html/urea_text.htm

4 Paul Spinrad, *The RE/Search Guide to Bodily Fluids*. RE-Search Publications, 1994, 50-54

5 Nsikan Akpan, Artificial sweetener reveals how much pee is in the average pool, PBS News Hour, March 3, 2017

6 Chloramines: Understanding "Pool Smell," https://chlorine.americanchemistry.com, July 2006

7 Carol Steinfeld, *Liquid Gold: The Lore and Logic of Using Urine to Grow Plants*, Green Frigate, 2007

8 John Gregory Bourke, *Scatologic Rites of All Nations*, Washington, D.C., W.H. Lowdermilk & Co., 1891 (also available in many reprints)

9 Auto-Urine Therapy (Shivambu Kalpa): The Indian version as detailed in the Damar Tantra, http://www.hps-online.com/hindiasutra.htm

10 Auto-Urine Therapy (Shivambu Kalpa): http://www.healsa.co.za/PDF%20Files/Damar_Tantra.pdf

11 C. S. Rayudu, *Drink Urine and Live Healthy*, New Delhi: GenNext Publication, 2016

12 Ibid, 43

13 Gaius Valerius Catullus, Kenneth Quin ed., *Catullus: Poems*, Toronto: Bloomsbury, 1973, 17-21

14 Neri Livneh, The Good Father, *Haaretz*, May 30, 2002

15 Henk van Doremalen en Paul Spapens, *Kruikezeikers. Mythe en werkelijkheid van een Tilburgs fenomeen,* Tilburg: Stadsmuseum, 2004

16 Laura Fry, The Fulling Story: All About Fulling Wool, www.craftsy.com/blog/2014/06/fulling-wool/

17 Miko Flohr, *The World of the Fullo: Work, Economy, & Society in Roman Italy*, Oxford Scholarship Online, 2013

18 Joe Schwarcz, Roman Laundry Secrets, *Montreal Gazette,* June 3, 2017, b5

19 Sally Magnusson, *Life of Pee: The Story of How Urine Got Everywhere*. London: Aurum Press Limited, 2010, 88-90

20 History of Woad, http://www.woad-inc.co.uk/history.html

21 Adam Hart-Davis and Emily Troscianko, *Taking the Piss: A Potted History of Pee*. Stroud, Gloucestershire, UK: The Chalford Press, 2006, 72-74

22 Margreta de Grazia and Peter Stallybrass, The Materiality of the Shakespearean Text, *Shakespeare Quarterly*, 44 (1993), 281–82.

23 Walter Mahan Jackson, *The Story of Selma*, Decatyr, Alabama: The Birmingham Print Company, 1954

24 http://wanette.k12.ok.us/activity drug policy.htm

25 Charlene Laino, Drug Tests Often Trigger False Positives, http://www.webmd.com/drug-medication/news/20100528/drug-tests-often-trigger-false-positives#1

26 https://www.oyez.org/cases/2001/01-332

27 JW 22315, www.marijuana.com/community/threads/how-female-pass-observed-urine-test-with-sythetic-urine.174305/

28 Ruth Harvey, The judgement of urines, *Canadian Medical Association Journal*, 1998;159, 1482-4

29 Ibid.

30 Ibid.

31 Roy Porter, *Quacks - Fakers & Charlatans in Medicine*, Stroud, Tempus, 2003, 181-186

32 Sniffing' urine to detect prostate cancer could prevent unnecessary biopsies, American Chemical Society News Release, April 3, 2017

33 The first full study of this subject is the fine and affecting book by Ida Macalpine and Richard Alfred Hunter, *George III and the Mad-business* (New York: Pantheon Books, 1970).

34 David H. Dolphin, *Porphyria, Vampires, and Werewolves: The Aetiology of European Metamorphosis Legends*, Paper given at the American Association for the Advancement of Science, 1985

35 Brett Bodner, Fifty Shade of Yellow, *New York Daily News,* April, 12, 2017

36 Roger Catlin, The Unknown Designer of the First Home Pregnancy Test Is Finally Getting Her Due, *Smithsonian.com*, September 21, 2015

37 Bruce Webber, Urinetown Review, *New York Times*, September 21, 2001

38 Stephen Halliday, *The Great Stink: Sir Joseph Bazalgette and the Cleansing of the Victorian Metropolis* (London: Sutton Publishers, 1999)

39 Ronald H. Blumer, *Wiped: The Curious History of Toilet Paper*. Middlemarch Media Press, 2013. 70

40 Alecia P. Long, General Butler and the Women, *New York Times,* June 18, 2012

41 Regency Hygiene: The Bourdaloue, *Jane Austen's World blog*, 2012 https://janeaustensworld.wordpress.com/2012/07/16/regency-hygiene-the-bourdaloue/

42 Sally Magnusson, *Life of Pee: The Story of How Urine Got Everywhere*. Aurum Press Ltd, 2010, 21

43 Henry Miller, *Black Spring*. New York: Grove Press, Inc., 1963, 51

44 Jon Henley, Mais wee, monsieur: Paris finds eco solution to public peeing, *The Guardian*, Feb, 1, 2007

45 Mark Davis, *The Atlanta Journal-Constitution*, December 20, 2013

46 Winnie Hu, A Public Restroom Fit for Brooke Astor Gets an Upgrade, *New York Times*, April 5, 2017

47 David Fleming, When athletes gotta go ... where do they go? *ESPN, The Magazine's Body Issue,* 2017

48 Jane Vorster, This is how marathon runners have a sneaky pee during a race, *South Africa News24*, March 8, 2016. An interview with the runner, Ryan Sandes

49 Miguel Llanos, Urine trouble states warn truckers, *NBC News*, 6/ 2/ 2005

50 NASA Environmental Control and Life Support System, Water Recovery System, *NASA technical report server*, Document #MSFC-0005604, 2007

51 Havelock Ellis, *My Life*, Houghton Mifflin Co., 1939

52 Jennifer Eve Rehor, Sensual, erotic, and sexual behaviors of women from the "kink" community. *Archives of sexual behavior*, *44*(4), 825-836.

53 Denson, R. (1982). Undinism: the fetishization of urine. *Canadian Journal of Psychiatry. 27*(4), 336.

54 Kafka, M. P.. The DSM diagnostic criteria for fetishism. *Archives of Sexual Behavior*, *39*(2), 357-362.

55 Sigmund Freud, *Civilization and Its Discontents*, tr. James Strachey. Norton, 1989. pp. 42-43

56 Doctor Mark Griffiths, *Urine demand: A beginner's guide to urophilia*, https://drmarkgriffiths.wordpress.com

57 Roland Oliphant, Vladimir Putin: "Our prostitutes are the best in the world, but I doubt Donald Trump would fall for them," *The Telegraph*, Jan. 17, 2017

58 Author's translation.

59 https://skipthegames.com/articles/escort-resources/an-escorts-guide-to-water-sports

60 http://torpedotheark.blogspot.com/search/label/uk%20law

61 http://www.wetset.net/index.php

62 Francois Rabelais, *Gargantua and Pantagruel,* Book one, chapter 17, author's translation.

63 Johnathan Swift, *Gulliver's Travels*, Part one chapter 5.

64 https://www.youtube.com/watch?v=3a5S6s55G7E

65 Bob Colacello, *Exposures*, New York: Putnam Publishing Group,1980.

66 www.christies.com/lotfinder/Lot/andy-warhol-1928-1987--oxidation-painting-5074062-details.aspx

67 Deborah Meyers, *Vancouver Sun*, February 25, 2015

68 Ibid.

69 Ellen Jong & Annie Sprinkle, *Pees on Earth*, New York: PowerHouse Books, 2006.

70 Ted Gott, *Don't leave me this way: art in the age of AIDS*, National Gallery of Australia, 1994, 93

71 Travis M. Andrews, Behind the right's loathing of the NEA: Two 'despicable' exhibits almost 30 years ago, *Washington Post*, March 20. 2017

72 www.sothebys.com/en/auctions/ecatalogue/2014/contemporary-art-day-sale-n09142/lot.496.html

73 http://www.christies.com/LotFinder/lot_details.aspx?intObjectID=6018093

74 Benjamin Sutton, http://blog.artinfo.com/artintheair/2013/12/25/a-brief-history-of-piss-christ/

75 Andres Serrano, Protecting Freedom of Expression, from Piss Christ to Charlie Hebdo, *Creative Time Reports*, http://creativetimereports.org, January 30, 2015

76 Michael Brenson, Andres Serrano: Provocation and Spirituality, *New York Times*, Dec.8, 1989

77 Ilan Stavans & Jorge J. E. Gracia, On Desecration: Andrés Serrano, Piss Christ, *Michigan Quarterly Review*, Volume 52, Issue 4, Fall 2013

78 Alan Axelrod, *The Real History of World War II: A New Look at the Past*, Sterling, 2008, 326

Made in the USA
Columbia, SC
21 October 2021